HB Playwrights
Short Play Festival 1999

THE AIRPORT PLAYS

HB Playwrights Foundation, founded in 1965 by Herbert Berghof and Uta Hagen, has provided an artistic home to more than 130 playwrights since it first opened its doors. Thirty-seven years, 270 full productions and countless staged readings later, it still makes available a safe and nurturing environment where theater artists come to work, free of the pressures of commercial theater. At the HB Playwrights Theatre, admission is free and critics are not invited so, playwrights, assisted by the actors, directors, designers, and other theater artists who volunteer their time, are free to take risks solely for the sake of their art. The Annual HB Short Play Series is one of the great success stories born of the artistic spirit first put into motion by Herbert and Uta so many years ago.

Robert Callely, Managing Director, HB Playwrights Theatre

OTHER BOOKS IN THE SERIES

HB Playwrights
Short Play Festival 1999
THE AIRPORT PLAYS

Edited by William Carden

CONTEMPORARY PLAYWRIGHTS SERIES

A Smith and Kraus Book

A Smith and Kraus Book
Published by Smith and Kraus, Inc.
177 Lyme Road, Hanover, NH 03755
www.SmithKraus.com

Manufactured in the United States of America

Cover and Text Design by Julia Hill Gignoux, Freedom Hill Design
Cover Illustration by Lisa Goldfinger

First Edition: December 2002
10 9 8 7 6 5 4 3 2 1

Contemporary Playwrights Series ISSN 1067-9510
ISBN 1-57525-285-6

CONTENTS

INTRODUCTION

The Airport Plays is the third collection of short plays written for a single location by members of the Playwrights Unit at the HB Playwrights Foundation and Theatre. The introduction to the initial volume, *The Motel Plays,* tells the story of how our annual event was developed by this unique group of writers. Most of the contributors to *The Motel Plays* and *The Museum Plays* are also represented here. It is fascinating to see where the special qualities of this location lead them in terms of form, content, and style.

An airport is a contained and suspended world, a public place that often serves as a catalyst for very private experiences. It is a place where we can be surprised by what happens to our consciousness when we have to wait. The prospect of travel — moving from a familiar place to the unknown or back to a place you once called home — can threaten our identities or liberate us from the assumed confines of our daily lives. As a result, these plays are full of the unexpected. We find characters afraid to get on a plane because suddenly the thought of what awaits them at the other end sends them reeling into the past. Other characters struggle to say an ordinary good-bye as they realize in their hearts that it is really a last good-bye. When they find themselves suspended between two places, strangers connect in surprising ways — while for others an encounter with an unknown foreigner creates the fear and attraction that forces them to confront their own assumptions.

Travel also makes us wonder, it makes us dream, and it can expand our sense of time. So more than before, these writers are drawn to move back and forth in time. People journey toward the future and into the past. In one play, unbeknownst to us, the characters are on their way to the hereafter. Another is bleakly set in the future after a nuclear holocaust. While there is a fair share of humor, existential themes prevail. Like travel itself, these plays challenge us with the unexpected and serve to sharpen our sense of what it means to be alive.

Once again, for the original production here at HB, we presented all the plays, dividing them into two programs that alternated for the course of the run. The single set designed by Andy Warfel along with the lighting designed by Chris Dallos imaginatively used familiar shapes to create the feel of an airport without literally being an airport. The design included elements that moved so the space could be reconfigured to represent the different parts of the airport in which the plays are set. While the individual plays can be performed on their own, they have a unique cumulative power when presented as a whole.

William Carden
Artistic Director

DEPARTURES

by Neena Beber

*To my grandparents, Lillian and Meyer Beber,
and Sally and Nathan Sacks — in memory*

ORIGINAL PRODUCTION
Departures was directed by David Simonds with the following cast:
Jane . . . . Pamela Gray
Pauline . . . . Julia Mueller

PLAYWRIGHT'S BIOGRAPHY
Neena Beber's plays include *The Dew Point, Hard Feelings, A Common Vision, Tomorrowland, The Brief But Exemplary Life of the Living Goddess,* and *Failure to Thrive.* Theaters that have premiered her work include The Magic Theatre, New Georges, The Women's Project, Theatre J (Washington, D.C.), Padua Hills Playwrights Festival, Workhouse, Urban Empire, The Ivy Theatre (L.A.), En Garde Arts, Echo's Ojai Theatre Festival, and Gloucester Stage. *Jump Slash Cut* received the L. Arnold Weissberger Award in 2001. *Misreadings,* a ten-minute play commissioned and produced by Actors Theatre of Louisville's Humana Festival, is included in *The Best American Short Plays 1996–1997* (Applause). An evening of her short pieces, *Acts of Desire,* premiered at Watermark Theatre. The short film *Bad Dates* (Touchstone) was based on her one-act *Food,* published in *Facing Forward* (Broadway Play Publishing). She has received an A.S.K. Exchange to The Royal Court Theater, an Amblin Commission from Playwrights Horizons, an Otterbein Commission, a MacDowell Colony Fellowship, and a Distinguished Alumni Award from NYU's Tisch School of the Arts, where she was a Paulette Goddard Fellow for her MFA. B.A., Harvard University. She is a member of New Dramatists, The New York Playwrights Lab, The Women's Project, and, with gratitude, the HB Playwrights Foundation.

CHARACTERS
    PAULINE, the younger sister.
    JANE, the older sister.
    (There is also the recorded voice of an airline attendant.)

DEPARTURES

Pauline and Jane sit with their bags in an airport waiting area. We hear a boarding announcement as the lights come up.

VOICEOVER: We'd like to welcome passengers seated in rows twenty-five to thirty-five to begin boarding. Rows twenty-five to thirty-five on flight 132, please proceed onboard . . .

(Pauline and Jane begin to exit. Jane continues offstage. Pauline freezes beside her carry-on bag. She clutches her boarding pass. She takes a step forward, stops again. After a moment, Jane wheels her bag back over to Pauline.)

JANE: What happened to you? Come on . . .

(Pauline doesn't move.)

JANE: What are you doing? We have to board now. Pauline. What? What is the matter, we have to go.

(Pauline turns from her sister and addresses us.)

PAULINE: Our grandmother was a wingwalker with Captain Sam's Flying Circus in the 1920s, when flying was still new. Three thousand feet up, she'd walk out onto the wings of biplanes to perform handstands and somersaults.

JANE: Pauline? What is *wrong* with you?

PAULINE: Sorry.

JANE: Sorry?

PAULINE: I — can't.

JANE: Can't *what?*

PAULINE: Can't do it.

JANE: What are you talking about?

PAULINE: I — I don't know what's —

JANE: Come on.

(Jane takes her arm and pulls her. Pauline resists.)

JANE: What? You don't want to go back home.

PAULINE: It's not that.

JANE: You're having some kind of premonition? This plane is going to crash or something? Don't tell me. Don't tell me, Pauline. I am getting on this plane, Pauline, and I am *getting* on this *plane,* and if you are having some kind of weird premonition that's going to give me anxiety even though I know you aren't psychic, even though I know you cannot predict the future and there is no way — well, keep it to yourself.

PAULINE: No, it's not . . . I mean the plane seems — fine. It's . . . suddenly . . . this . . . *(Turning out again.)* Jane loves fish. Not eating them. Looking at them. She and my father, both — fish lovers. Dad used to take us snorkeling in the Keys, and we'd hover together over coral reefs, watching each other watching. And then one year, suddenly, just like that, I was afraid of swimming with fish.

JANE: We are going to get on this plane, Pauline. Come on.

PAULINE: I wish — I could.

(Jane starts to go, stops.)

JANE: Do you want me to get on without you? So just force yourself. How can you do this now?

PAULINE: I'm not doing — on purpose — this — shit. I don't know what's happening. It's this overwhelming — physical — impossibility, my getting — on.

JANE: Two thousand tons rising thirty thousand feet into the sky is a physical impossibility. Your walking from here to there — I'm sorry, but I don't see the problem.

(Pauline tries. Stops again.)

JANE: For Dad.

PAULINE: Dad won't be there.

JANE: He's not gone yet.

(Jane sits, defeated. Takes out a pack of cigarettes and puts a cigarette in her mouth, removes it.)

JANE: I can't believe they've all gone nonsmoking. Do you want a mint?

(Jane searches in her bag for a mint. Another boarding announcement, underneath.)

VOICEOVER: Passengers seated in rows eleven to twenty-four may now board. Rows eleven to twenty-four, please have your boarding passes ready.

PAULINE: You should get in the line.

JANE: We have a minute.

PAULINE: You don't need to sit here with me.

JANE: Oh. Now. Now that I'm sitting here. It's not for you, Pauline. It's for me. Do you think it's easy for me to go back? To see Dad, knowing . . . knowing that he's not — well? Do you think it's easy for *Dad?* But it's always you, it's always you who needs to be taken care of.

PAULINE: *(Out.)* I'm the youngest. When you're the youngest you always feel . . . young. And that the oldest is old. Even when she's eight. Because when you're six, eight's old. Always older.

(Jane grabs her wallet, gets up.)

JANE: Do you want anything?

PAULINE: *(Out.)* I never let Jane be the young one. I was the young one. *(To Jane.)* Are you sure you have time?

JANE: No. We don't have time. I want a mint.

(A boarding announcement.)

PAULINE: Maybe we should call him.

JANE: Let him sleep. It's earlier there.

(Jane goes.)

PAULINE: All my life, Dad's been at the other end of every journey. Sleep-away camp, Aunt Carol in Chicago, Teen Tour, backpacking in Europe, college, weddings, holidays, bringing home Nick . . . Dad always waiting at the airport, hours early, waiting to pick us up.

(Jane comes back with mints. She is reading a magazine. She sits.)

PAULINE: *Natural History?* Did you get anything good?

JANE: *(Sitting.)* Shit.

PAULINE: What?

(Jane begins to sob.)

JANE: The parrot fish has been put on the endangered species list. It's the coral reefs. They're dying off. Coral is a living thing, it has to grow, and we're — every day — killing it off, killing the coral reefs, the — shit —

(Pauline looks to Jane, not sure how to comfort her.)

PAULINE: *(Out.)* Sand dollars. Bags full of them. I mean literally. Dozens. We waded through the shallow part to collect them. Fuzzy brown things. Like pancakes. We took them home, boiled them with Clorox to bleach them bone white. For decoration, you know. Everyone did it. You wouldn't know they were a living creature. There was absolutely no evidence of it. *(Looking to Jane, who is still crying over the magazine.)* Suddenly, one year, I was afraid of swimming with fish. Suddenly I was afraid.

(Thunder and lightning. A beach, sometime in the past.)

PAULINE: We have to go back.

JANE: Not yet. More shells.

PAULINE: I'm going.

JANE: It's just rain, Pauline. Dad says it's okay.

PAULINE: Lightning, people die of lightning, Jane . . . People die.

(Back to the present.)

(Jane goes back to the magazine, crying. Pauline turns to us. Out.) Our grandmother was a wingwalker in the early days of flight, when people still believed it was some sort of miracle, and I used to dream of tottering on

the wings of biplanes, finding my balance up in the clouds. It's hard to say when it happened, when I became afraid of . . . everything.

(A scary sound. A kid's room, sometime in the past. Pauline runs to Jane.)

JANE: Jesus. What are you doing?

PAULINE: I heard something.

JANE: It's just night noises, Pauline.

PAULINE: What are night noises?

JANE: They're the same as day noises but you hear them better at night because there aren't other competing noises. Like a house, when it settles, it creaks. And cats, well, they make more noises at night because our night is their day. And —

(A loud crash. They hug each other, scared.)

PAULINE: Should we wake Dad?

JANE: It was just the garbage can. A raccoon knocking over the garbage can. That's all. Where are you going?

PAULINE: To wake Dad.

JANE: Don't. Dad hardly gets any sleep, Pauline. Leave Dad alone.

(Back to the present.)

(Jane closes the magazine, crying.)

PAULINE: It's just coral, Jane. *(Out.)* I never know how to comfort Jane. Jane was always the one who comforted me, I never — *(Back to Jane.)* Maybe we can send in money. The coral's not all going to die. Is it?

JANE: Everything goes away.

PAULINE: *(Out.)* Time travel. Jane used to try to explain it to me, but I could never understand it. If you can go back in time, doesn't that mean that the past always has to exist, alongside the present? Dad's face when he was sixty-five, fifty, forty-five, forty . . . I can see him so clearly, waiting for us to arrive. The past, a parallel reality, on-and-on on a loop, waiting to be re-entered at any moment, like a black hole — turbulence. *(To Jane.)* Thanks for driving.

JANE: What?

PAULINE: For always being the one to drive.

JANE: I like to drive.

PAULINE: I like being driven.

JANE: *(Pulling herself together.)* Works out beautifully, then.

VOICEOVER: Rows six to eleven and all first-class passengers who have not yet boarded, please proceed through the gate with your boarding passes ready.

JANE: Let's get on. Come on, Pauline.

(*Another airport, sometime in the past. Pauline is at the top of an escalator, Jane at the bottom.*)

JANE: Come on.

PAULINE: I'm going to fall.

JANE: What is your problem? You've been on escalators before.

PAULINE: I'm going to lose my balance, Jane.

JANE: Just step on. Slowly. Come on, Dad's waiting. I'll come back up and hold your hand, okay? Dad's right down there . . .

PAULINE: (*Out, urgent.*) All my life my sister led me forward, while my father waited patiently on the other side.

JANE: (*Younger, waving.*) Over here, Dad!

PAULINE: How long have you been here, Dad?

JANE: Daddy! Dad! Over here . . . Dad . . .

(*Back to the present.*)

PAULINE: (*Out.*) Our grandmother was a wingwalker in the 1920s, for nearly a decade. When our father was born he ended her career with Captain Sam's Flying Circus, and, consequently, she spent the rest of his childhood with her head in the clouds while he wandered, unprotected and alone, on the ground. He gave my sister and me the kind of childhood he would have liked to have had.

VOICEOVER: All remaining passengers for flight 132, please board at this time.

JANE: I'm getting on. Are you coming or not?

(*Pauline looks at her, not moving forward.*)

JANE: So don't come, Pauline. Avoid the lightning. Avoid the stingrays and the night noises and the down escalator —

PAULINE: How did you — ?

JANE: — the ocean and the germy toilets and the high diving board. Avoid it all, stay protected, do whatever you need to do to feel safe. (*Starts to go.*) I'll take care of Dad. I'll make up an excuse for you. Go ahead; turn around and give up.

PAULINE: I'm not afraid of flying. I'm not even afraid of dying.

JANE: What, then?

PAULINE: I'm afraid of landing.

JANE: Landing?

PAULINE: (*Out.*) I used to think that clouds had weight and substance. When we flew through a field of clouds, I really believed that if we could open the exit doors, we would be enveloped by soft pillows . . .

JANE: (*Remembering, to herself.*) Marshmallows . . .

PAULINE: *(To Jane.)* I couldn't understand that those perfect safety nets were just — vapors.

JANE: *(After a beat.)* Maybe he will be there, Pauline.

PAULINE: You think so?

JANE: Maybe he's having an exceptionally good day.

VOICEOVER: This is the final boarding opportunity for flight 132. Flight 132, this is your final boarding opportunity.

(Jane looks at Pauline. Pauline hesitates, then rushes off to board the plane with Jane. Blackout.)

END OF PLAY

STORKS

by Catherine Filloux

To John Daggett

Storks was directed by Jean Randich with the following cast:

Anne .... Julie Fain Lawrence
Mamilou .... Victoria Boothby
Man .... Joel Garland

PLAYWRIGHT'S BIOGRAPHY

Catherine Filloux's new plays, *Silence of God* and *Mary and Myra,* premiered at Contemporary American Theater Festival (CATF) in 2002 and 2000. *Mary and Myra* also appeared at Todd Mountain Theater Project in 2002. Ms. Filloux is the 2003 James Thurber Playwright-in-Residence. She has been commissioned for a new play by Theatreworks/USA. She wrote the libretto for the opera *The Floating Box,* which received its world premiere at the reopening of Asia Society in 2001 (composer Jason Kao Hwang). Her first play, *Cut To: The Deal,* was produced in Theater X's 2002 season. Ms. Filloux is the winner of the 1999 Roger L. Stevens award from The Kennedy Center Fund for New American Plays for her play *Eyes of the Heart* and is the winner of the O'Neill's 1996 Eric Kocher Playwrights Award. She developed *Eyes* for Lifetime TV. *Photographs from S-21*, from the "The Museum Plays," was a finalist for the 1999 Heideman Award at Actors Theatre of Louisville and is the winner of the 1999 Nausicaa Franco-American Play Contest; it has been produced in Paris, England, Phnom Penh, and around the United States. *Storks* was produced at HB Playwrights Foundation and in the Immigrants' Theater Project's "Women without Borders Festival" at the Lower East Side Tenement Museum Theater. *Lessons of My Father* was part of "The Funeral Plays," at HB Playwrights. *The Sun Always Rose* was in "New Georges: Watch This Space," at HERE. *The Price of Madness* was produced by Emerging Artists at INTAR on Theatre Row; *Three Continents* appeared at New Georges; and *The Russian Doll* at Lincoln Center Theater Directors Lab. *White Trash* (1997 Heideman finalist), *Accepting Applause,* and *Converting* were staged at the Women's Project. *All Dressed Up and Nowhere to Go* and *Venus in the Birdbath* were produced in Baltimore and Buffalo. Ms. Filloux has developed an oral history project, *A Circle of Grace,* with the Cambodian Women's Group at St. Rita's Refugee Center in Bronx, New York. She was awarded a 2001 Artist's Residency Grant from the Asian Cultural Council for playwriting in Phnom Penh, Cambodia. She received her French baccalaureate in Toulon, France, and her MFA from the Dramatic Writing Program at New York University. She is a member of New Dramatists.

CHARACTERS

ANNE, a woman in her thirties.

MAMILOU, the woman's French grandmother; she is a regal woman, with a white fur hat.

MAN

PLACE

JFK Airport.

TIME

Present.

NOTE

"Je te vois voler
Au-dessus de la mer
Pour retourner
Vers ton pays
Pays de ton coeur
Pays du soleil
Oh, Algérie!"

"I see you flying
Above the ocean
To return
To your long lost home
The land of your heart
The land of your sun
Home again."

STORKS

JFK Airport in New York. Mamilou, a regal woman, with a white fur hat, sits awkwardly at a table, off a fast-food place, with Anne, thirties. Right near them is an airplane gate. Anne takes small kiwi tarts from a New York bakery bag and arranges them on the table. Mamilou speaks with a French accent.

ANNE: I forgot to bring spoons.

MAMILOU: *Oh, mon dieu!*

ANNE: How will we eat without spoons?

MAMILOU: I don't know . . .

ANNE: I bought the tarts in New York. I walk by the bakery every day, I thought of you. I didn't think of the spoons, and the place here only has forks . . . Do you think we could eat them with forks?

MAMILOU: Well, that's certainly not an easy prospect . . .

(Anne arranges tea, purchased from the fast-food place and looks through some packets.)

ANNE: I'm sorry . . . Mami, do you want sugar in your tea?

MAMILOU: *Oui*, a small teaspoon.

ANNE: There's only sugar substitute . . .

MAMILOU: *(As if a foreign entity.)* "Sugar substitute?"

ANNE: It's like saccharine. Not real sugar. People use it for diets . . .

MAMILOU: *(In near horror.)* Diets? . . . Oh, no, no, never. Thank you.

ANNE: Do you want milk?

MAMILOU: Just a drop, please.

ANNE: It's from a packet . . .

MAMILOU: No, then. Thank you.

ANNE: Maman and I always meet here. When she goes to see you in France, when she comes back. It's the only place . . . We always sit, she gives me the news, shows me pictures, brings me the lavender water . . .

MAMILOU: *Ah, oui* . . .

(Mamilou clutches a rather large, severe black bag on her lap.)

ANNE: Do you want to put your bag down?

MAMILOU: No.

ANNE: I can hold it. So it's out of your way? I'll be careful.

(Mamilou continues to clutch it.)

ANNE: Do you want to take off your sweater? Aren't you hot?

MAMILOU: *(Firmly.)* No.

ANNE: We're going to be here for a while. You should be comfortable.

MAMILOU: I told your mother they could have just escorted me from one plane to another, it would have been much simpler. Wasn't it too difficult for you to come?

ANNE: No, it was easy, I took a bus. I do it all the time. It's simple . . .

(Mamilou looks around.)

MAMILOU: The man, he will return with the wheelchair, you are sure?

ANNE: He said he'd be back. He promised. He looked very dependable.

(Mamilou sighs.)

MAMILOU: I didn't know. He spoke only English. He had a receding chin. Well, he'll be here anytime. It will be time to go . . .

ANNE: We do actually have a little time together, before he comes.

(Anne hands her a plastic fork.)

ANNE: Here. You know, in America, people eat dessert with forks.

MAMILOU: No!

ANNE: They do.

(Mamilou sighs, looking at her watch.)

MAMILOU: My watch is still on California time. It's nine hours later in France?

ANNE: Yes. It's three in the afternoon here in New York.

MAMILOU: *(Resetting watch.)* I'll set my watch to French time. In France they're about to go to sleep.

(Anne picks up her tart.)

ANNE: I guess I'll just eat the tart with my fingers . . .

(Anne shows her, taking a bite. Mamilou looks at the plastic fork.)

MAMILOU: Are you sure the man will return?

ANNE: Yes. *(Annoyed.)* It's not time yet.

MAMILOU: *(An aside.)* He had an unattractive face.

ANNE: What do you mean?

MAMILOU: His face was unattractive.

ANNE: That's actually not very nice.

(Mamilou is completely honest and unmoved.)

MAMILOU: I don't mean anything nice or *not* nice, by it. It's just the truth.

(Mamilou opens her black bag.)

MAMILOU: I brought you some food from the plane, they give you so much. *(She reassures herself, looking through bag.)* My ticket and passport are right here. Your mother gave me a little American money just in case, before I arrive back in France.

ANNE: You won't need it . . .

(Mamilou takes out some little packages of food from the plane.)

MAMILOU: *Du camembert, du chocolat, et une pomme* . . . I couldn't eat it . . .
   (Anne takes the little packages, now more annoyed.)

ANNE: Maman probably paints some pretty bad scenarios, but I'm not starving. I just want you to know that. I'm not starving. *(Looking at the little plane packages.)* Thank you, that was very nice, to save the food . . .

MAMILOU: *(Lost in memory.)* They treated me very nicely. Your mother had spoken to everyone, they all knew who I was. At every turn, "Madame Piovanacci, may I help you with this? Are you comfortable here?"

ANNE: Did you exercise your legs a little?

MAMILOU: *(Sighing.)* Well, it's almost time . . .
   (Anne tries to hide her sadness and anger.)

ANNE: Fine, all right, it's almost time.
   (Mamilou looks at her as if she's crazy.)

ANNE: Maman called me twice today. She's worried she should've accompanied you back to France.

MAMILOU: It would have been simpler.

ANNE: I was right here. I *live* here . . . I wanted to see you . . .

MAMILOU: *(Sighing.)* The second part of the trip is always longer.
   (Mamilou tries to cut a piece of the tart with the plastic fork, but doesn't succeed.)

ANNE: You want me to cut it? *(A moment of abandon.)* You know, you could just pick it up with your fingers. How hard would that be?
   (Mamilou simply stares at the tart.)

ANNE: *(Aimlessly.)* . . . There's a lot of vitamin C in Kiwi.

MAMILOU: Kiwi?

ANNE: It's an Australian fruit.

MAMILOU: Australian?

ANNE: From Australia. *(Impatiently.)* You know what Kiwi is.
   (Mamilou just stares at the tart. The two women are at an impasse.)

ANNE: So are you looking forward to getting back to France?

MAMILOU: Everyone's gone.

ANNE: What do you mean, everyone's gone?

MAMILOU: Everyone's gone. Your grandfather, all my friends. *(Confiding.)* You know, I can't bring myself to respond to letters. People write to me and I don't write back! I didn't answer any of the Christmas cards I received this year.

ANNE: You don't have to *answer* Christmas cards.

MAMILOU: *Oh, oui,* Anne, you do have to answer. Those nice neighbors who live across from your mother's, they wrote to me. I would like to respond but I know no English and I could get no one to help me.

ANNE: What do you want to say? I'll write it.

MAMILOU: "Thank you for your generous wishes. Please excuse the extreme delay of this card."

(Anne writes it on a napkin.)

ANNE: Here . . . You never wanted to learn English?

MAMILOU: No . . .

ANNE: All these years you've come to the United States? Never wanted to communicate with the people?

MAMILOU: No . . . And the housework, I let things go.

ANNE: Why not? You deserve it. Take it easy.

MAMILOU: The dust, everything's filthy . . . And I barely cook for myself.

ANNE: What do you like to eat? What makes you happy? You used to like chocolate . . . ?

MAMILOU: Nothing. Everyone's gone. Your grandfather . . . *(Looking around.)* That man is late.

(Anne faces Mamilou straight on.)

ANNE: Look, as far as I'm concerned you don't have to do anything you don't want to do, anymore. Just relax.

MAMILOU: Oh, I *should* do things.

ANNE: Who says?

MAMILOU: I don't know.

(After a beat, Anne takes out a Scrabble game.)

ANNE: Have you been playing a lot of Scrabble? *(Scrabble is always pronounced with a French accent.)*

MAMILOU: With myself, not very enjoyable.

(Anne hands her a bag with the letter tiles in it.)

ANNE: Here, we don't have much time. Pick a letter, so we can figure out who goes first.

(Mamilou doesn't pick a tile. Anne does.)

ANNE: Okay, look, I got an "O." Worth one point, you're winning already. Pick a letter.

(She holds out the bag.)

MAMILOU: We cannot play Scrabble. In an airport? . . .

ANNE: Of course, in an airport! People *always* play Scrabble in airports. *(Improvising.)* At least in America.

MAMILOU: They do?

ANNE: New York is the Scrabble capital of the world.

MAMILOU: *(Pouting.)* When you play in English it's not the same.

ANNE: *(Firmly.)* I'm playing in French . . . If I played in English I'd probably beat you.

(Mamilou looks at the board.)

MAMILOU: This is the English version, the letters aren't worth the right amount of points . . .

ANNE: *(Holding out the bag.)* Remember how many "Scrabbles" you got last time we played? Pick a letter. Actually, it was amazing how many Scrabbles you came up with.

MAMILOU: *Oui,* it *is* amazing. I'm very good.

(Mamilou picks her letter from the bag.)

MAMILOU: *(With great satisfaction.)* Zed! That's worth ten points. I'm first.

ANNE: I can't believe it! *(Handing her the bag.)* Pick six more letters. Last time your scores were in the three hundreds . . . My mother says, sometimes you cheat.

MAMILOU: No.

ANNE: You use those sheets. That give you words for the hard letters?

MAMILOU: Those are allowed . . . My friends allowed them . . .

(Mamilou dumps her letters back into the bag.)

MAMILOU: I don't feel like playing. *I hate Scrabble.*

ANNE: *(Shocked)* What?

MAMILOU: *I loathe Scrabble* . . . Your grandfather was the one who always cheated. He'd hide his tiles, if he didn't like them. *(With great delight.)* Mostly he had fun disrupting the game! He was a real rebel . . . Oh, no! I nearly forgot the lavender water for you!

(Mamilou takes a bottle from her black bag.)

ANNE: Thank you.

(Anne opens the bottle and slaps some water on her cheeks.)

ANNE: It always reminds me of him. It smells so good.

MAMILOU: *Oui,* he would put it on after he shaved, every morning.

(Anne looks out the window.)

ANNE: Look, it's finally sunny — winter's about to end! It's a beautiful day in New York. Look!

(Mamilou looks out the window and continues to look.)

MAMILOU: *(Unsure.) Oui,* really?

ANNE: For you, the *sun,* Mami. It came out for you.

MAMILOU: Well, I don't know.

ANNE: You love the sun!

MAMILOU: I'm not so sure . . .

ANNE: Sunflowers! Remember the bouquet in the room where I used to sleep at your house. In the Van Gogh poster?

(Mamilou lets out one of her distinctive sighs.)

MAMILOU: It goes so fast . . .

ANNE: What Mami, what goes so fast?

(Mamilou goes to the window, staring out at the bright sunlight — transfixed. Anne follows, surprised.)

MAMILOU: Do you know something, Anne? At the age of sixteen your grandfather decided to stop going to school . . .

ANNE: Oh.

MAMILOU: He became a winemaker, and on top of the wine house where he worked there was a minaret where storks made their nests. Every year the storks flew to *Algérie* for the winter, because the climate was gentler there than in France. The wine house was called the House of Storks — *Dar el Askri* in Arabic . . .

ANNE: You speak Arabic?

MAMILOU: Yes . . .

ANNE: I didn't know.

MAMILOU: *Oui,* a little. Later, your grandfather joined the 33rd *Régiment d'Aviation* and his unit was called The Storks. He wore the emblem on his left shoulder. Once, he came home from his sister's house with a baby stork that had fallen from its nest. The stork set up on our terrace and we fed her fresh fish — she cackled to say hello and thank you.

(The sunlight becomes progressively brighter.)

MAMILOU: But at the end of winter the little stork flew away towards France with the other storks. Over the blue Mediterranean, the Camargue with its marshes filled with frogs to eat, over the prairies, the villages, in the IMMENSE sky. All the way back to the nests of the older storks, perched high up on French chimney tops.

ANNE: Like you, now. Flying home.

MAMILOU: No, France wasn't our home. We were from *Algérie.* After we were forced to leave, your grandfather always missed it so much.

ANNE: And you?

MAMILOU: *(Looking outside.)* I missed the sun.

(Anne takes her hand.)

MAMILOU: My hands are rough.

ANNE: Your nails are pretty.

MAMILOU: No.

ANNE: . . . I never do mine.

MAMILOU: You should.

(The two women stand at the window holding hands, looking out. A man with a wheelchair enters.)

ANNE: The man is here.

(He reads from a piece of paper.)

MAN: "Madame Piovanacci"?

ANNE: *(Going to him.)* Yes, thank you for coming back.

MAN: I'm true to my word. *(He points off.)* Other people needed the chair . . .

(The man and Anne help Mamilou make the transfer to the wheelchair.)

ANNE: She can walk, it's just when she's flying , my mother says it's better this way . . .

(Anne hands Mamilou her black bag.)

MAMILOU: *(Patting them.)* Ticket . . . passport. *(To Anne.)* Here, take my American money, I don't need it . . .

ANNE: No.

MAMILOU: *Oui,* for the bus.

(Anne takes the money.)

ANNE: Thank you, Mamilou. *(To the man.)* Her name is Marie Louise, but we've always called her Mamilou . . .

MAMILOU: Well . . .

ANNE: It's time to go . . .

(Anne leans down.)

ANNE: In all honesty, *I've* never heard of anyone answering Christmas cards. Just let it go . . .

MAMILOU: One *does* need to answer, but suddenly I *can't.*

(Anne holds her grandmother close.)

ANNE: I'm saying good-bye, now. Mami?

MAMILOU: The man is here.

ANNE: You look so good in that hat, I *love* that hat.

MAMILOU: Always the same, I've had it for so long . . .

ANNE: It's hard to carry off such a hat!

MAMILOU: *(Dismissing her.)* Now, now . . .

(Anne clings to her grandmother, as the man stands, unsure.)

ANNE: I can't say good-bye.

MAN: . . . We like to take the passengers who need special assistance first . . . We need to get her settled . . . She needs to come now . . . You don't want her to miss her plane? . . . *It's time.*

(Anne lets go of her grandmother.)

ANNE: Mamilou? . . . *Au revoir.*

(The Man starts to push Mamilou away. Mamilou can't contain herself and turns back.)

MAMILOU: *Ma petite . . .*

(The man pushes her toward a shaft of light, which represents the gate. It becomes brighter as Mamilou disappears and Anne stands. After a moment the man comes back from the shaft of light, pushing the empty wheelchair. Anne looks at the empty chair. The light at the gate and the sunlight at the window become brighter and brighter.)

END OF PLAY

THE AIRPORT PLAY

by Alexandra Gersten-Vassilaros

The Airport Play was first produced at the Herbert Berghof Playwrights Theater in June 1999; directed by Caroline Kava with the following cast:

Hari . . . . Harsh Nayyer
Anne . . . . Caitlin Clarke

THE AIRPORT PLAY

A woman is sitting on one side of a small row of seats in an airport waiting area. The woman is American, in her thirties or forties. She is reading a self-help book, Ten Steps to True Love. *In the background, for a few moments we hear the sounds of a television tuned to CNN.*

An Indian man of similar age approaches the bench. He is well dressed in a dark suit. He speaks with an Indian accent. He sits near her. She is aware of him and perhaps perturbed by his close proximity. He makes himself comfortable and causally, as is his gentle way, watches her read. She finally looks at him.

MAN: My plane is delayed. *(Beat.)* And you.

WOMAN: I'm reading.

MAN: Your flight?

WOMAN: They're cleaning it.

MAN: I see.

WOMAN: Excuse me.

MAN: Pardon?

WOMAN: Excuse me.

MAN: Ah. Ah. Certainly.

(She resumes reading.)

MAN: I find these televisions hanging from the ceiling quite intruding. Every opportunity to contemplate the world interrupted by talking boxes. *(He sighs.)* And the air. It's old. Old air. Very old.

(Woman clears her throat pointedly.)

MAN: I'm flying to HOUSTON. *(Pronounced "Howston.")* Where are you flying?

WOMAN: I'm sorry, but I'm not really comfortable talking with strangers at airports.

MAN: Why? Strangers can be objective and reassuring, most especially at airports. There is always a sense of development, change, isn't it? We are *coming* from somewhere and *going* to someplace else, do you see? We are departing. We are arriving. Don't you find, Miss-I-don't-know-what-your-name-is?

WOMAN: *(Concentrated agitation.)* I don't mean to be rude or *American,* but I've had a very difficult, um, *year,* and I'm trying to soothe myself with a book before I reboard.

MAN: Go on, Miss. I am so sorry. Of course.

WOMAN: Thank you. *(She opens her book to read. He notices the cover, Perturbed — a beat.)*

MAN: That is Omkar Nath Cardiramani's book, isn't it?

WOMAN: Hmmmhmmm.

MAN: What page are you on?

WOMAN: Um. *Two.* I'm on page, uh *two.*

MAN: Chapter?

WOMAN: *One.* Page two. Chapter one. You see? I've only just begun. *(She resumes reading. A beat.)*

MAN: It looks as if you are eating the book with your eyes. As if your eyes had teeth and you are devouring each word.

WOMAN: Look, sir . . . I'm just trying to sit here until I reboard, as I've said, and, well, relax, do you mind?

MAN: I'm sorry, I do.

WOMAN: Excuse me?

MAN: I do mind, Miss. I do mind!

WOMAN: You are beginning to disturb me, sir.

MAN: Yes, I sense that, Miss, nevertheless I am disturbed myself.

WOMAN: Clearly.

MAN: Miss-I-don't-know-what-your-name-is . . .

WOMAN: I'm not going to tell a disturbed man my name, if that's what you're after.

MAN: All I want, Miss —

WOMAN: I don't care what you want!

MAN: May I finish?

WOMAN: No. I want to read my book.

MAN: May I please finish, Miss —

WOMAN: I'm not telling you my name. Are you some sort of creep?

MAN: No, Miss, I am a fine man. I am. There is no need to become alarmed.

WOMAN: I want to read. You won't let me read!!

MAN: I want only for you to stop reading *THAT* book. Any book but that.

WOMAN: I don't know you. You don't know me. I want to read what I want to read. It has nothing to do with you.

MAN: Please, no.

WOMAN: Please no? Please no?

MAN: It has very much to do with me.

WOMAN: I have a whistle in my bag, sir.

MAN: It is a SELF HELP book, is it not?

WOMAN: I'm not ashamed. Yes. I need help. I'm helping myself.

MAN: But the man who wrote it hasn't got it.

WOMAN: Hasn't got what?

MAN: Self, Miss. No self. None to be found.

WOMAN: How do you know?

MAN: I know.

WOMAN: *(Impatient.)* You know what?

MAN: I know the man. That man there. *(Points to photo on back cover.)*

WOMAN: You know him. You've met him? He's a friend of yours?

MAN: No longer a friend. He has stolen my wife, Miss.

WOMAN: I'm sorry?

MAN: I am going to my brother for heart surgery in Houston. *(Pronounced Howston.)*

WOMAN: This is a "con-artist at the airport scam," isn't it? I'm supposed to give you cash so that you can pay for heart surgery.

MAN: No, Miss. I am a rich man. I own a rubber factory.

WOMAN: So? So what?

MAN: Because of that man my heart is broken in pieces. I have actual pains in my chest. *(He takes out a handkerchief and wipes his brow.)* I'm having one now. *(He takes a pill from a small box.)*

WOMAN: *(Becoming concerned for him.)* I don't believe this.

MAN: He has no self, Miss. Trust me. This man is dangerous. He has taken my wife from me. Stolen her.

WOMAN: People go. They're not stolen. Anyway he's married with children.

MAN: He has left *his* wife and children to be with *my* wife and children.

WOMAN: Are you mistaking this man for someone else? This man is a big celebrity.

MAN: Yes.

WOMAN: He's admired all over the world.

MAN: I know.

WOMAN: He has his own institute.

MAN: But he has *no self!*

WOMAN: What? What does that even mean?

MAN: It's a fact.

WOMAN: "No self??"

MAN: It is true, on my oath —

WOMAN: I don't believe you. I have all his books!

MAN: I'm quoting him! He has said this, out loud to my person. One stormy evening in Ooty, on a porch in Southern India, we were sitting on a small swinging loveseat under a red canopy, overlooking a great blue hill . . .

WOMAN: Uh huh . . .

MAN: He had a drink in his hand. He was swilling the alcohol around the perimeter of the tumbler, then he downed the contents like a bear, turned to me and growled; "I have no self!"

WOMAN: I'm sorry, I'm finding this very hard to believe . . .

MAN: Yes! Because the "SELF" is his calling card. His claim to fame.

WOMAN: I have all his tapes! I belong to his Serenity Club.

MAN: I wondered if this most bizarre confession was for him an epiphany, perhaps resulting in the production of more books, better books.

WOMAN: I get bimonthly newsletters!

MAN: Instead he laughed, Miss. A condescending guffaw ridding himself of recognition entirely.

WOMAN: It just seems so unlike him So unlike his newsletters.

MAN: The he returned to the bar to refill his tumbler with more grain alcohol. Indian alcohol. Brown and blinding.

WOMAN: My God! He drinks too?!?

MAN: He's bloated, greasy, and foul!

WOMAN: He doesn't look bloated in this photo.

MAN: Trick photography.

He has pulled the wool over many eyes including his own.

WOMAN: What about your wife?

MAN: She was in the powder room when all of this occurred. I had gone to his home on the hill to convince her to return to me. Thank heavens my children are grown.

WOMAN: *(Reading the title of the book.)* Ten Steps to True Love.

MAN: HA! He knows his love is false. *This* is the crime. The crime against my wife. Against you.

WOMAN: It's fraud, isn't it? It's worse than fraud.

MAN: *(He wipes his tearful eyes.)* Walking through this airport has been a living hell, with his book staring at me, his peaceful expression taunting me, Miss, from every cash register at every candy stand. Appalling. And then to see you intently reading . . . I do hate him. I do. No I don't. Yes I do. No, I don't. Wait. Wait. I love him because he is a fellow human being, and human beings, I believe, are capable of extraordinary growth but he disappoints his potential constantly. *(He wipes his eyes again.)* And my wife. He disappoints her as well. I have letters. In my briefcase. She tells me he beats her.

WOMAN: He beats her?! Omkar Nath Chardiramani beats his wife?!!

MAN: My wife. He beats the beauty out of her. She loves him still.

WOMAN: My God!

MAN: She writes this. My heart breaks more as we speak.

(He blows his nose into the hankie)

WOMAN: God, I'm so sorry. I really am.

MAN: You must listen to your own self, Miss. Not the borrowed nonsense of this criminal. You have many stupendous ideas of your own.

WOMAN: I do? *(Beat.)* Where?

MAN: Right there, to be sure. *(He points.)* In your heart.

WOMAN: Thank you.

MAN: Give me the book.

WOMAN: What are you going to do with it?

MAN: I'm going to shut it. *(He shuts it abruptly. He looks at it.)* I'm going to rip it. *(He tries.)*

WOMAN: Can't I just return it?

MAN: *(Still trying to rip it in half. He cannot.)* No, please.

WOMAN: It was twenty-five dollars.

(Voiceover: Delta Flight 234 to Milwaukee boarding all passengers at gate fourteen.)

MAN: I don't want anyone to read it, ever ever ever again!

WOMAN: You're upset.

MAN: I'm upset with myself. I should have known.

WOMAN: Known what? What could you have known . . .

MAN: I did know!!

WOMAN: Be easy on yourself.

MAN: I tried to *please* her.

WOMAN: My flight's starting to reboard. I don't want to leave you like this.

MAN: I felt always kind of Mephistophelian war in my stomach. I loved her, but I knew it wasn't entirely good . . . I always suspected. The body speaks but we don't listen.

WOMAN: No one listens. Who listens? I don't listen.

MAN: It was as if the first moment attached me to her with concrete. Concrete!

WOMAN: How did you meet her?

MAN: It was at a banquet. She was wearing a violet sari, standing beside a column of plates, a small dish of cake in her hand.

(He shows her a photo from his wallet.)

WOMAN: She looks like a princess.

MAN: Indeed, she is a princess.

WOMAN: Really?

MAN: A daughter of a maharajah.

WOMAN: How could you resist a princess?

MAN: Her face had the expression of a statue in a temple. However, she was not nearly as serene as I'd projected.

WOMAN: Projection, yeah. I've been through the mill myself.

MAN: What mill is that?

WOMAN: Oh it's an expression, The mill. That's why I bought this book.

MAN: Oh. Because of "the mill." *(He is sad.)*

WOMAN: I'm sorry. If I'd known I wouldn't have bought it.

MAN: Thank you. I thought love was something, Miss, that I'm just *today* realizing it's not.

WOMAN: I know. It's not. It's not what?

MAN: It's not suffering.

WOMAN: It's not?

MAN: It's not.

WOMAN: I thought it was.

MAN: No.

WOMAN: Oh, good. *(Truly wants to know.)* What is it, then?

MAN: *(Little laugh.)* Well, it's much more complex to say what love *is* . . .

WOMAN: Yeah.

MAN: But it's not ah —

WOMAN: No, you're right. It can't be —

MAN: Yes, no.

WOMAN: Not just . . .

MAN: Suffering.

WOMAN: No.

MAN: No.

WOMAN: I'm learning . . .

MAN: Slowly.

WOMAN: I'm older, I should know.

MAN: The years are hidden behind your liveliness.

WOMAN: I don't feel lively.

MAN: Your *potential* for liveliness.

WOMAN: I like to laugh, I do, but it's been a long . . .

MAN: We must be kind to each other, isn't it? ["Isn't it" is an Indian locution for "don't you agree?"]

WOMAN: I'm in the throws of, well, I've just walked out of a very . . . I *knew* at the start it was . . . well, actually, *he* walked out on *me* . . . he didn't walk really, he sort of ran, my God. This morning he told me my face was sad and that it oppressed him.

MAN: He makes you unhappy and so your face shows this unhappiness and he punishes you for your face even though . . .

WOMAN: He started it.

MAN: Nobody starts it. But someone must end it.

WOMAN: Well, *he* did. That doesn't make it easier.

MAN: One hates their job and so they are fired, isn't it?

WOMAN: Oh yeah, I see what you mean.

MAN: We wait, We wait for the tide to shift despite —

WOMAN: —our own —

MAN: You see!

WOMAN: — so stupid, isn't it.

MAN: Time passes us by, *digitally* now, and we lose our . . .

WOMAN: — *life!* Isn't that what you were going to —

MAN: Yes. We lose —

WOMAN: Our life —

MAN: We fail to answer the call.

WOMAN: *(She calls out.) LIFE!*

MAN: We enthrall ourselves to the wrong person —

WOMAN: And we become petite. We —

MAN: — shrivel and lose moisture —

WOMAN: Pleasers. Hopers.

MAN: Alert and anxious.

WOMAN: You know, I called him twenty-eight times from every bank of phones in this airport, smashing out his office number *hoping*, hoping he'd come and apologize for hating me, for hating my face.

MAN: Your eyes are lovely. Their shape is almond.

WOMAN: I think that's because they're swollen.

MAN: Nevertheless. We have tried to love the unlovables.

WOMAN: You're right. You're absolutely . . .

MAN: They don't want love, isn't it?

WOMAN: You're right. It's not.

MAN: Absolutely.

WOMAN: We should probably bless them . . .

MAN: Yes, yes! "I love you, but be elsewhere."

WOMAN: "I love you but be elsewhere!" I love that!

MAN: Are we going to rise to the occasion of our lives?

WOMAN: We're not kickballs, we're not napkins . . . we're, we're —

MAN: ME.

WOMAN: I'm —

MAN: You!

WOMAN: You're —

MAN: *Yes! (Exuberant.)* We have to rise to the occasion of —

WOMAN: Rise. Address ourselves —

MAN: Yes!

WOMAN: — like buglers or something —

MAN: *(Trumpeting sound.)* PATA PATA!!!

WOMAN: And and and and . . .

MAN: Thrive.

WOMAN: Absolutely.

MAN: Yes!

WOMAN: That is such a good word!

MAN: Yes.

WOMAN: Yes. *(Beat. Quieting down.)* I'm sorry for being rude earlier.

MAN: You are forgiven six times over. By the way, what is your name?

WOMAN: Oh. Anne. Anne with an E. The E is silent.

MAN: But *you* are not. *(Announcing as if she was a queen.)* You are ANNE.
    WITH AN E. The pleasure is mine. My name is Hari. With an "I."
    (They shake hands.)
    *(Voiceover: This is the final call for Delta Airlines flight 234 to Milwaukee.
    Final boarding call for Delta flight 234 to Milwaukee.)*

WOMAN: Oh my, I think they just . . . that was me.

MAN: Dear me . . . I have kept you . . .

WOMAN: Not at all. I wasn't listening —

MAN: Yes, neither did I —

WOMAN: *(Gathering herself.)* I have enjoyed speaking with —

MAN: It was a —

WOMAN: Gosh, I'm sorry to —

MAN: It was most —

WOMAN: Oh, God, oh, it was so —

MAN: Anne —

WOMAN: Oh God, I wish . . .

MAN: I wish . . .

WOMAN: I thought it would be —

MAN: Before the —

WOMAN: Yes . . .

MAN: But —

WOMAN: It was —

MAN: — rejuvenating —

(Another handshake.)

WOMAN: Yes. Rejuvenating. It —

MAN: Yes. Anne —

WOMAN: I'd — Hari.

MAN: Anne —

WOMAN: Better —

MAN: Yes.

WOMAN: Bye. (She exits.)

MAN: Bye. (He waves.) Bye!

(Another man enters the stage. He sits. He picks up the book that the woman left behind. He reads. Hari approaches and notices the man reading. Hari sits, closes his eyes. The sounds of CNN reemerge, airport announcements, etc. Hari clasps his hands simply and breathes deeply in meditation. Ravi Shankar music begins and gets louder as the lights fade.)

END OF PLAY

I AM LAIKA

by Dmitry Lipkin

To all those stressed-out pets

I Am Laika was directed by Shira Piven with the following cast:

Airport announcement . . . . Sheryl Moller
Female dog . . . . .Tami Dixon
Male dog . . . . David Prete
Woman-form . . . . Jessica Allen
Man-form . . . . Richard Rodriguez

PLAYWRIGHT'S BIOGRAPHY

Dmitry Lipkin was born in Moscow and emigrated to Louisiana at age eleven. His plays include *Cranes* (produced by The New Group, 1999), *Skitaletz, "The Wanderer"* (O'Neill National Playwrights Conference, 2000), *Moscow Nights* (A Contemporary Theatre, Seattle, 2000), *Baton Rouge* (EST), *The Elephant Play* (Playwrights' Collective, Printer's Devil Theatre), *Pithecus, I Am Laika,* and *The Tightwad,* (HB Playwrights), *A Forest of Stone, My Job is My Life* ("Chekhov Now" Festival, NYC 2000), and *Incident at Dental Clinic #44* (a screenplay for Fox/Searchlight). Mr. Lipkin is a recent alumnus of New Dramatists, an MFA graduate from NYU, a past Van Lier Fellow at Manhattan Theatre Club, and the 2000 Bug 'n Bub award-winner from Primary Stages. He has taught playwriting at NYU and is a co-founder of The Playwrights' Collective (1990–1998), with whom he produced a ton of new work off-off-Broadway in a very small room. After finishing his play *The Poet's Hour,* Mr. Lipkin spent most of 2002 in southern Mexico where he studied Spanish, wrote his new play *Total America,* and ate a whole lot of avocados.

NOTE

I Am Laika is a play of fun and mischief and, I think, should be treated with fun and mischief. Whatever emotions its desolate landscapes may evoke, it is after all only a play, and a short one at that.

I AM LAIKA

"What Time Is Grey," by Phillip Glass, is blasted at full volume. Lights rise. An airport. The stage is bare, with the exception of two large pet transport carriers, spaced at least several feet apart. Their entrances face upstage, and very little, if anything, of what is happening inside the carriers is seen. On the intercom we hear the distant steady voice of airport announcement.

AIRPORT ANNOUNCEMENT: Flight fifty-nine, departing for Los Angeles, now boarding in gate eight. Flight fifty-nine, departing for Los Angeles, now boarding in gate eight.
(This continues, distant, in a loop.)
(Carrier one shifts a bit, as we feel the movement inside of it. A male voice comes out of it — Male dog.)
MALE DOG: You're hungry?
(Carrier two also shifts a bit. A female voice comes out of it — Female Dog.)
FEMALE DOG: Very much.
MALE DOG: I'm hungry very much as well.
FEMALE DOG: It seems like it has been forever, hasn't it.
MALE DOG: It does.
FEMALE DOG: And you know what? I'm nauseous very much as well.
MALE DOG: I'm nauseous too. Although we haven't even boarded yet.
FEMALE DOG: Why do you think we're nauseous then?
MALE DOG: . . . I do not know. *(Silence.)* You've vomited?
FEMALE DOG: Too much I am afraid.
MALE DOG: Me too. As well as . . .
FEMALE DOG: — I don't need to know.
(Silence.)
MALE DOG: What . . .
FEMALE DOG: Yes?
(Silence.)
FEMALE DOG: What breed, you want to ask?
MALE DOG: Just as a point of curiosity.
(Silence.)
FEMALE DOG: What breed are you? *(Pause.)* You can lie, you know.
MALE DOG: I know.
FEMALE DOG: But would you want to — is the question, isn't it.
MALE DOG: Let's keep it democratic.

FEMALE DOG: All right. Democratic then. *(Silence.)* How long do you think it has been?

MALE DOG: I cannot tell.

FEMALE DOG: It . . . seems so long . . .

MALE DOG: Interminably long.

FEMALE DOG: I mean, for this type of a thing . . . Which shouldn't take so long at all . . . *(Pause.)* Have you . . .

MALE DOG: . . . Been in the carrier before? A long long time ago.

FEMALE DOG: So . . . ?

MALE DOG: It is hard for me to gauge . . . how it was then . . . compared to . . . *(Pause.)* If I had, perchance, a clear sight of the sun, or if there were a set of meals . . . for me to measure time with . . .

FEMALE DOG: But there is nothing! That is what I'm trying to say!

MALE DOG: It is kennel time. In length, the feeling is akin to kennel time.

FEMALE DOG: This is no kennel time I know. *(Pause.)* And the voice.

MALE DOG: The voice?

FEMALE DOG: The lady . . . She's not making any sense.

MALE DOG: How can you tell?

FEMALE DOG: She is saying the same thing over and over. Like she's trying to train herself. No lady I have ever known has ever done a think like that.

MALE DOG: Maybe she is . . .

FEMALE DOG: What?

MALE DOG: Trying to train herself. *(Pause.)* Maybe we can help.

FEMALE DOG: No lady that I know has ever tried to train herself.

MALE DOG: But still —

FEMALE DOG: — "Still" not, my breedless friend.

MALE DOG: I never said —

FEMALE DOG: — You might as well have. That's all right.

MALE DOG: . . . And you . . . ?

FEMALE DOG: I'm rootless as I am.

(They share a quiet laugh. Pause.)

MALE DOG: We are together then?

FEMALE DOG: Together . . . ?

MALE DOG: In our rootlessness.

FEMALE DOG: Together and apart. As we have been.

(Silence. Lights fade a bit on the carriers.)

AIRPORT ANNOUNCEMENT: *(Fading up.)* Flight fifty-nine, departing for Los Angeles, now boarding in gate eight. Flight fifty-nine, departing for Los Angeles, now boarding in gate eight. *(She sighs.)* The truth. *(Pause.)* As far as truth exists. Is that no one has boarded much of anything in quite some time. Yes, naturally, I go on. Keep on announcing flights, departures, destinations, airlines, the like, but as it stands, the bulk of it is useless information. Yes. I do it and will keep on doing it because as you may or may not have gathered, I am prerecorded. I can't help myself.

(A dry chuckle.)

I'm doing and will keep doing what my maker had already done. M maker, being a stocky woman named Louise, alas now petrified, the chalky substance of her bones now swirling in the Newark air, mixing with others that have met her fate, which is to say, the world, the whole fan-fucking swirling world. The population of the planet swirling in the air as I sit snug inside my loop, inside my tape. Cocksuckers all of them. But I digress.

(Silence.)

What happened as you might have gathered, is the bomb. Alas, the bomb. Where it all started — that I cannot say. I'm prerecorded after all. But rumors point to a republic in the former eastern bloc. From there, it spread, enveloping each country, throttling and burning every soul. Alas, the bomb is not a toy.

(She sighs.)

And now, in the middle of el Carnival, the world is silent. It is February after all. The Tri-State area is cold. There's snow or bone dust on the ground, rivers are frozen, howling winds . . . Between my useless infinite announcements I had ample time to think . . .

(Silence. Her tone has changed.)

And thought I have . . . Though what about I can only . . . Well . . . Not that I'm not allowed to or can't but somehow . . . inasmuch as I, a part of me, is capable of . . . that is, I'm afraid.

(Silence.)

At any rate. I am at peace with it.

(She segues into her announcement, then back —)

AIRPORT ANNOUNCEMENT: Flight fifty-nine, departing for Los Angeles. Flight fifty-nine, departing for Los Angeles. /This isn't and will never be/ Flight fifty-nine, departing for Los Angeles, now boarding in gate eight /my fate. My fate!/ Flight fifty-nine / my fate! / Flight fifty-nine, departing for /this isn't and will never be!/ . . . now boarding in /my fate/ . . . Los Angeles.

(She goes into a quiet loop, as —)

FEMALE DOG: What would you do if you had been a man?

MALE DOG: If I had been a man, I'd love you very much.

FEMALE DOG: But you had never even seen me . . . !

MALE DOG: I've been close to you for quite some time. I hear your voice. I think of you. If I had been a man, I'd love you very much.

FEMALE DOG: And yet, you're not a man.

MALE DOG: I could be if I want it to be so.

FEMALE DOG: *(Sad.)* And yet . . . I'm not a woman.

MALE DOG: You could be a woman.

FEMALE DOG: How?

MALE DOG: You make yourself a woman. Like I make myself a man.

FEMALE DOG: . . . You first.

> *(Silence. We hear him strain.)*

MALE DOG: I can't . . . I think that I can only be man . . . if you are there . . . to *see* me as a man.

FEMALE DOG: And I would have to be a woman, I suppose.

MALE DOG: Yes, you would have to be a woman then.

> *(Silence.)*

FEMALE DOG: Your logic has a lot of holes. Because as you need me to see you as a man, I would need you, to see *me* . . .

MALE DOG: As a woman.

FEMALE DOG: Yes.

> *(Silence.)*

MALE DOG: . . . Destined, we are, to drown in the night.

> *(Silence.)*

FEMALE DOG: Unless.

> *(Pause.)*

MALE DOG: Unless what?

FEMALE DOG: Unless we aren't at sea. Unless this is an island, or a raft. A place where we could swim to and be safe.

MALE DOG: . . . Then we are far?

FEMALE DOG: Not too far. We can see the island in our sight.

MALE DOG: On the horizon?

FEMALE DOG: Closer.

MALE DOG: Closer . . . Then we'll need a rope.

> *(Silence.)*

FEMALE DOG: What do you mean?

MALE DOG: First comes the rope, and then come we. If we approach the island from two sides, we use the rope to hoist ourselves into the land. If I pull on the rope and you do not, the rope falls in the sea and so do I, and you as well.

FEMALE DOG: And if *I* pull, and you do not . . .

MALE DOG: Again, the rope falls in the sea. But . . .

FEMALE DOG: Yes.

MALE DOG: If we pull . . .

FEMALE DOG: Yes . . .Yes . . . Yes.

MALE DOG: . . . So then, this *is* what we attempt?

FEMALE DOG: First comes the rope.

MALE DOG: The rope.

(Lights shift as we now notice a rope, lying half hidden in the debris, with either end disappearing on opposite sides of the stage.)

MALE DOG: We have the rope . . . And now we need to pull.

(From either side, the ends of the rope are slowly lifted off the ground by unseen hands.)

MALE DOG: You're pulling?

FEMALE DOG: Yes. And you?

(Slowly, the rope is lifted off the ground and becomes taut. Their voices, also, tighten up.)

FEMALE DOG: I know you're pulling. I can feel you pull.

MALE DOG: And I, can you.

FEMALE DOG: Do not let go, my friend.

MALE DOG: I won't.

FEMALE DOG: *(In pain.)* I . . .

MALE DOG: Yes . . . I know . . .

(Two pairs of hands become visible on either side of the stage, slowly making their way up the rope. They are followed by two pairs of feet.)

FEMALE DOG: There . . . I think . . . we are coming on.

MALE DOG: Don't look. First close your eyes.

FEMALE DOG: First . . . close . . . the eyes . . .

(Two human forms, man and woman, appear on either side of the stage — their eyes closed, clutching onto the rope. Their appearance is monstrous, as if their features had been compiled and stitched together from a thousand different sources. Yet there is also a wonderful goodness, innocence . . . whatever attire they have should probably remain black and white.)

FEMALE DOG: We're there you think?

MALE DOG: I cannot tell.

(The human forms stop, remain motionless, holding onto the rope. Silence.)

FEMALE DOG: Should we . . . ?

MALE DOG: I . . . I'm afraid . . . What if . . .

FEMALE DOG: What if?

(Pause.)

MALE DOG: You go on.

FEMALE DOG: I can't. It's both, or neither one.

MALE DOG: . . . At once then?

FEMALE DOG: Both at once.

(Pause. Slowly and simultaneously, the human forms open their eyes, turn their heads towards each other, fix their gaze. Silence.)

FEMALE DOG: And so, I'm a woman.

MALE DOG: . . . And so, I'm a man.

(The forms remain frozen, as we become aware of the distant announcement loop.)

AIRPORT ANNOUNCEMENT: *(Indignant.).* Cocksuckers all of them. Cocksucker you, the listener, in particular.

(She sighs.) "Yet as there are no listener, cocksucker none" . . . "Cocksucker all have gone away." Cocksucker, I am all alone. Cocksucker, help me, someone, anyone. Cocksucker, please.

(She is seized by a horrible fear.) I am degrading, gradually. Literally . . . My voice, which is in essence — me — is fading and destabilizing slowly from the basic pain of overuse. I'm hoarse. I die from talking too damn much.

(A dry chuckle.) And yet, I cannot stop. The flights, arrivals and departures, gates, times, cities long destroyed, cocksucking useless information of cocksucking useless buried world is going through me, eating me alive! . . . What can I do? I try to stop, but it's not in my power *to* stop . . . ! It's like . . . if I contained a virus, only to discover that the virus was myself . . . ! What am I then to kill? . . . And who am I to salvage? Who am I to save . . . ?!

(Silence) I guess . . . there is a part of me that feels a great amount of guilt and, I suppose, responsibility for . . . well, I'll say it, I'll just say it — for destroying it . . . the world.

(Pause.) Not that I did it. Or had anything to do with it, but in as far as I am representative, or part of general . . . You know what I am trying to say . . .

(Earnest.) I don't think that it was a good thing for the human being To be apart from who they were. To have their thoughts so splintered, rendered meaningless . . . And inasmuch as I am . . . what is rendered . . .

(We hear coughing, vomiting, as the dogs become sicker and sicker, closer to death. The forms remain frozen, clutching the rope.)

AIRPORT ANNOUNCEMENT: . . . I am Laika.

(She fades. The dogs' voices are now halting, tired.)

MALE DOG: Are you all right?

FEMALE DOG: Are you?

MALE DOG: Not much.

FEMALE DOG: . . . And so, am I.

MALE DOG: Yet we are on this island. Sun, and sand!

FEMALE DOG: I feel a bit too sick to move myself.

MALE DOG: You want to try?

FEMALE DOG: I don't know if I can.

MALE DOG: *(Trying to cheer.)* Try.

FEMALE DOG: I . . . I'll try.

> *(The woman-form jerks up her head and hand. The movement is robotic, strained. She briefly holds it up, trying to make a second move, then gives up as the head and hand fall back.)*

MALE DOG: Here . . . Let me help.

> *(The man-form jerks his body, trying to maneuver the hips. There's a lot of movement, signifying nothing and yielding little result. When he finally does set a course, it is away, not toward her.)*

FEMALE DOG: You aren't . . . coming toward me.

MALE DOG: I'm not?

FEMALE DOG: You are away from me . . . Going away from me.

> *(The man-form hits a wall.)*

MALE DOG: I've hit myself.

FEMALE DOG: A tree perhaps?

MALE DOG: A palm tree, yes.

> *(The man-form shakes, trying to caress his head, robotically.)*

FEMALE DOG: Poor you.

MALE DOG: Poor . . . poor poor me.

FEMALE DOG: I . . .

MALE DOG: Yes?

FEMALE DOG: I want to kiss your head . . .

MALE DOG: . . . My head?

FEMALE DOG: I . . . want to kiss . . . where there is pain in it. *(Silence.)* Can I?

> *(The man-form begins to move toward her, awkwardly, though less awkwardly than before.)*

MALE DOG: I'm . . . I am coming toward you.

> *(He gains speed, coming directly toward her.)*

FEMALE DOG: Stop.

> *(Man-form stoops, abruptly, nearly knocking her over. Pause.)*

MALE DOG: . . . I have stopped.

FEMALE DOG: . . . Don't tease me now.

(Slowly, with great difficulty, the woman-form begins to lift her head. She opens her eyes, fixes her gaze on the man-form, standing beside her.)

FEMALE DOG: Where is it, the pain?

(The man-form points at his forehead. She leans in, kissing the empty space nearby.)

MALE DOG: You've missed it. You have kissed the empty space.

FEMALE DOG: I'm sorry.

MALE DOG: Not your fault.

FEMALE DOG: . . . Guide me. *(Silence.)* Will you, my lips?

MALE DOG: Your lips, into my head?

FEMALE DOG: *(Sick.)* . . . Guide me my lips.

MALE DOG: I will.

(The man-form, shakily, lifts up his arms. He clasps her head then begins to draw it toward him with strained difficulty. He brings her lips up to his forehead, as she kisses it. Silence.)

FEMALE DOG: Have I now kissed the pain?

MALE DOG: . . . You have.

(Pause. She remains still, her lips on his forehead.)

FEMALE DOG: That's good. *(Her voice grows quiet, frail.)* . . . Now all is well.

(Silence. The forms remain still.)

MALE DOG: Are you . . . ? Can I . . . ? *(Silence.)* You want to touch my eyes?

(The man-form pulls back, looking at the woman-form, which remains still, her lips kissing the empty space.)

MALE DOG: Here. Touch my eyes.

(The man-form haltingly takes her limp hand, brings it to his eyes.)

MALE DOG: My eyes . . . ! You see. These are my eyes . . . !

(Silence. The man-form caresses her hand on his eyes. There is panic on his face.)

MALE DOG: You see? — My eyes! . . . You see — my eyes . . . !! *(Silence. He understands.)* And these . . . these are *your* eyes.

(He pulls her hand to her *eyes, moving it haltingly so as to caress them.*

MALE DOG: *Your* eyes.

(He lets go of her hand. It drops, limply. He looks at her, sad, and closes her eyes. From the carrier, a quiet weeping sound can be heard.)

("Labyrinth," by Phillip Glass, slowly fades up. There will be three elements to this, the final movement of the play — the music, the announcement, and the movement of the human forms. The three will overlap, with the important points of each drawn out for emphasis.)

AIRPORT ANNOUNCEMENT: *(Soft, pensive.)* I miss Louise sometimes. Her breath. The way she would infuse me with surprise, and how that basic chaos turned into a smile, and meaning. She was not particularly special, but she was — how can I say — alive. To pass the time between the flights, I tried to reproduce her thoughts. To be, or to play at being her . . . To think what she thought of the bomb . . . and of the fears and emptiness she felt, as she looked up into the sky . . .

(At this point, the man-form downstage begins to speak to us — in garbled broken syllables. He contorts, angry, in a great deal of pain, struggling to impart his garbled message, as —)

AIRPORT ANNOUNCEMENT: I miss her breathing life into my empty shell, her mind forever straddled with That Thought, her daughter on cocaine, her fantasies — her sex-filled wonder fantastic fantasies? — of men and islands, sand and fuck! Puerto Rican men squeezing her breasts as she infused me with the latest on the Stockholm flight . . . ! *(A laugh.)* That I suppose is what I miss. No, not the men, but possibility. The prism of seeing through her eyes, of thinking through her thoughts and feeling her! Feeling so much of her, a part of me.

(The man-form has said his piece. He leaves us be, walking upstage toward the woman-form, dancelike. As the announcement keeps on with an almost breathless ease, he dances a halting ritual around the woman-form, expressively trying to bring her to life.)

AIRPORT ANNOUNCEMENT: *(Open, emotional.)* As I am on my own I'm cold and dry . . . ! Yes, sure, there is a twinge of wit, a sparkle of emotion, basic stuff like fear of death or expiration, or the basic beastly stuff to chill your blood, but there's no . . . joy in me. No joy like she possessed. No joy of looking at the sun, even with daughter on cocaine, and husband Frank forever guzzling, itching to hit her and then hitting, once, twice, and with that knowledge looking at the sun and knowing . . . who she was. And where she was and knowing with that happy knowledge that she is alive . . .

(The woman-form moves her hand. He stops dancing, watches her. She jerks several times, coming alive.)

AIRPORT ANNOUNCEMENT: I, with no daughter on cocaine, and needlessly to say no husband hitting me, I, voice without aching back, without asthma, menstrual cramps, glaucoma and the like, experience no joy . . .

(The woman-form opens her eyes, looks at him, lovingly, knowingly, then slowly lifts up her hands.)

AIRPORT ANNOUNCEMENT: I live in memory and words. Words jumbled, rearranged, words that I strive to put into coherent meaning, but that have no meaning for me . . . Only for the listener that isn't there . . .

(The woman-form and man-form come together and join hands. They are no longer awkward, but joyous and graceful. They turn toward us.)

AIRPORT ANNOUNCEMENT: . . . the listener that I so long to meet . . . and give them meaning.

(The forms lift their hands to us in an open greeting.)

AIRPORT ANNOUNCEMENT: . . . Give me joy.

(The airport announcement softy sings the last line, as we fade.)

(Blackout.)

END OF PLAY

THE FLIGHT OF THE LAST CALHOON

A One-Act Play with Songs
by Quincy Long

PLAYWRIGHT'S BIOGRAPHY

Quincy Long's most recent productions include *The Lively Lad,* presented by New York Stage and Film at the Powerhouse Theatre at Vassar, and Soho Rep's production of *The Year of the Baby. The Joy of Going Somewhere Definite,* commissioned by the Mark Taper Forum, won a 1996 Fund for New American Plays Award and has been produced by the Atlantic Theater Company, the Mark Taper Forum, the Magic Theatre, and others. Mr. Long has recently adapted the play for Icon Productions in Los Angeles and has also adapted another play, *Shaker Heights,* which was nominated for an Outer Circle Critic's Award, for Atlantic Films in New York City. Mr. Long, who is from Warren, Ohio, and lives in New York City, was recently commissioned to write a play for Playwrights Horizons and for the Ensemble Studio Theatre/Sloan Foundation Science and Technology Project. He's a graduate of the Yale School of Drama and a member of the New Dramatists and the Ensemble Studio Theatre as well as the HB Playwrights Unit.

CHARACTERS
>   CALHOON, a middle-aged Irishman.
>   MALE SECURITY GUARD, thirties, black.
>   FEMALE SECURITY GUARD, thirties, black.

PLACE
>   Airport security.

THE FLIGHT OF THE
LAST CALHOON

*Lights up on Airport Security: a suggestion of the door-sized frame for peo-
ple to pass through and the boxy machine that scans their luggage. The appa-
ratus is staffed by two black security guards, one male, one female. Calhoon
enters with a suitcase and hesitates, nervously.*

MALE SECURITY GUARD: Want to pass your bag through, sir?

CALHOON: Excuse me?

MALE SECURITY GUARD: You coming through or what?

CALHOON: Is there a doctor? A doctor here?

MALE SECURITY GUARD: This the airport.

CALHOON: I've got to see a doctor.

MALE SECURITY GUARD: We got a dentist.

CALHOON: I'm afraid to get on the airplane.

MALE SECURITY GUARD: *(To female security guard.)* Nurse.
   *(Female security guard approaches with clipboard and wheeled chair. She seats
   Calhoon and hands him a clipboard.)*

NURSE: Name. Age. Insurance and etcetera, please.
   (Nurse fills shot glass as Calhoon fills out form.)

DENTIST: So, what seems to be the problem, Mr., uh, *(Looking over Calhoon's
   shoulder at form.)* Calhoon?

CALHOON: Well, I'm scared to death to fly, you know, but tomorrow's the
   funeral, so I'm up early, waiting for my taxi, when the wind starts buf-
   feting about the house, and the radio starts saying about accidents and
   how "even good pilots make mistakes."

DENTIST: Mm hm.

CALHOON: Then I hear a noise, the noise, and see a tremendous great airliner
   come crashing to earth, right flat down upon the ground and plowing
   off through the neighborhoods, sweeping all before it. Oh my goodness,
   what a terrible omen. I don't want to go to the airport, of course, but I
   have to, and what do I see when I get there but an ancient old fella col-
   lapsed upon the sidewalk, head cracked open, blood all over, staring right
   up in my eyes, holding up his hand to me. Oh doctor —

DENTIST: Nurse.

CALHOON: I'm deathly afraid to get on that airplane.

(Nurse hands Calhoon the shot glass as dentist examines clipboard.)

NURSE: Rinse.

(Calhoon takes a mouthful, gargles, swallows, and hands shot glass back to the nurse.)

DENTIST: You Mormon, Mister Calhoon?

CALHOON: I'm a tenor.

DENTIST: Uh huh.

CALHOON: The baritone's what I *wanted* to be.

DENTIST: Open, please.

(Calhoon opens his mouth. Dentist looks inside.)

CALHOON: See anything?

DENTIST: Not pregnant are you, Mr. Calhoon?

CALHOON: No, I'm not.

DENTIST: We'll take a picture, then.

CALHOON: Pardon?

DENTIST: We need some x-rays, Mr. Calhoon.

CALHOON: Oh.

(Nurse helps Calhoon to the baggage scanner.)

NURSE: Just lay down on the machine, please, sir.

(Calhoon lies down on the baggage scanner, putting his head through the flap. Dentist and nurse look at the monitor.)

NURSE: Head to the side, please, sir. Breathe and hold . . . now to the other side. Breathe and hold . . .

DENTIST: Yep. There it is. Lodged sideways in the alveolus.

CALHOON: *(From inside.)* See anything, then?

NURSE: You can come out now, sir. Thank you.

CALHOON: Was there anything there?

DENTIST: When did you eat last, Mr. Calhoon?

CALHOON: *(Sings.) This morning when I last did eat*
    I had a muffin and a beet
    And drank a coffee and a shot
    And took some pills and smoked a lot

DENTIST: Well you appear to have aggravated something.

CALHOON: Oh, my. Don't like the sound of that.

DENTIST: Do you know the story, Mr. Calhoon, about the man who had a fish embedded in his jaw?

CALHOON: No, no, I don't believe I do.

DENTIST: Well to put it in layman's terms, your wisdom tooth's come in a bit crooked.

CALHOON: I see.

DENTIST: Which prohibits its natural eruption, which causes abscess, which causes pain.

CALHOON: Have to come out then, will it?

DENTIST: We'll have to put you under.

CALHOON: Whatever it takes to get on that plane.

(Nurse stands behind Calhoon.)

NURSE: Give us your head, sir.

(Nurse takes Calhoon's head and sings an Irish lullaby as dentist puts on cap, becoming Irish father.)

NURSE: *When the snoozy dozy man*
Comes the chimney down
He brings his sack of dreamy dreams along
He puts you in his sack
And hoists you on his back
And carries you away to Oolagong

(Calhoon's head falls back. Nurse continues singing as she puts on a shawl, becoming Irish Mother, and Father puts glasses and an oversize cap on Calhoon.)

NURSE: *(Continued.) In Oolagong the streets and shops and houses are all yellow*
The cows and pigs and chickens are all green
Trees are pink and printer's ink is purple as
The passion
And memories are the color of gangrene

(Father leans in the door frame. Mother pokes at a frying pan on the baggage scanner, now a stove. Calhoon, now an Irish Lad, sits up in the chair in glasses and cap, his suitcase still beside him. Lights change.)

FATHER: "NICE FELLA. WASTE OF TIME." That's what'll be carved on yer stone.

MOTHER: It won't either.

FATHER: It will, ye know it will.

MOTHER: And what's it to you?

FATHER: They'll not be sayin' that o' the last of the Calhoons. No sir, he's goin' to America and not wastin' his time playin' mooncalf to the heifer next door.

MOTHER: "Like his old man afore him."

FATHER: Like his old man afore him.

MOTHER: "I coulda been a tradesman."

FATHER: I coulda, goddamnit!

MOTHER: As if that was the be all and end all.

FATHER: What the hell do you know? When did ye ever have to go out and make the world? When did ye ever have to do anything a'tall except go to the movie house and giggle with that pack o' darlins?

MOTHER: Oh don't start with me movies.

FATHER: Then shut up and get the lad his breakfast before he misses his airplane.

MOTHER: *(Working the fry pan.)* Goin' off all alone.

FATHER: And stop yer motherin' 'm for Christ's sake. Thirteen is near enough a man. Are ye afraid to go to America, boy?

LAD: No.

MOTHER: What do you expect him to say?

FATHER: Do ye not want to go to New York City and see the lights on?

LAD: Yes, I want to go to New York City.

FATHER: Well there ye are.

MOTHER: What a triumph.

LAD: But, I'm comin' back someday.

FATHER: By the time ye seen yer first stewardess ye'll have forgot all about yer little next-door Jenny.

LAD: I won't fergit her never.

MOTHER: Leave him alone.

FATHER: He can shift for himself.

LAD: And I'm comin' back, I say.

FATHER: You can come back when you've made somethin' of ye.

LAD: I'm comin' back for yer funeral.

FATHER: What?

MOTHER: Don't talk that, now.

LAD: And I'm gonna piss on your grave.

FATHER: Oh, ye've earned yerself a beatin' now.

LAD: Gonna put me on the airplane all beat up, then?

FATHER: I'll beat ye where it don't show. I'll beat the goddamn daylights outa ye!

MOTHER: Stop it now, the both of ye.

LAD: I'll say it again. I hate ye and I'm comin' to piss on yer grave.
   (Father slaps Lad. Mother claps hands as Lad turns head.)
   I'll piss on it every single day.
   (Father slaps Lad again. Mother claps hands as Lad turns head.)

LAD: I'll piss on it so religious the ground'll give way and yer coffin'll wash to the river and then to the sea and float to your precious America where you can raise up from the dead and get a flunky's job at the hotel, which is all ye've ever done and all yer fit for!

FATHER: *(Pulling his belt out of its loops.)* You steamin' pile of shite, ya.

MOTHER: Stop now.

FATHER: I'll have the hide off him. I will. Swear to God I will.

MOTHER: You apologize to your father.

LAD: I won't.

MOTHER: Ye get down on your knees to him and beg his forgiveness.

LAD: I won't! I won't! I hate him! I hate you!

(Father raises the strap. Mother intercedes.)

MOTHER: No, now!

(Father flings her back.)

FATHER: Get outa there!

LAD: Coward!

FATHER: Coward, is it?

(Father puts the belt around the Lad's neck and starts to choke him.)

FATHER: Bookish little bastard. I'll have yer neck off.

MOTHER: Stop! Stop it!

FATHER: I'll have ye beggin' for mercy. Go on. Beg fer it.

(Mother pulls at Father.)

MOTHER: Stop it! Yer chokin' him to death!

(Father throws Mother back with one hand and continues choking Lad with the other.)

FATHER: Say it! Say yer sorry!

(Lad is near to passing out. Mother seizes frying pan and mimes conking Father on the head. Father goes down. Mother and Lad stare down at him.)

MOTHER: Well, now we done it. *(Beat.)* Shake his hand.

LAD: What?

MOTHER: *(Holding unconscious Father's hand up.)* Shake his hand, now. I don't want yer goin' through life with it on yer conscience ye never forgive the man that made ye.

LAD: No. I won't. I can't.

MOTHER: Go on to America, then.

LAD: But what about you?

MOTHER: Don't be worryin' about me. *(He starts for her, arms out.)* No, no. Yer father and I are of a piece. I take his side. Always. Get on to Shannon with ye. Go on.

(Father stirs.)

MOTHER: Quick now. Before he awakens and murders ye.

(Father sits up.)

LAD: *(Startled.)* Ah!

(Father holds the frying pan in front of his face. The bottom of the frying pan is a mask painted to look like a suffering old man with a bloody face. Father stretches out hand to Lad in a pathetic gesture.)

LAD: Father?

(Mother sings.)

MOTHER: *Father's in his coffin*
His sins are in the past
So say good-bye and sorry
For time has come at last

(Lad takes Father's hand. Beat. Lad pulls Father up as lights change: Mother strikes shawl, caps, frying pan/mask and glasses and resumes identity as nurse. Father is now Dentist. Lad is Calhoon. Calhoon and Dentist are shaking hands.)

DENTIST: My pleasure, Mister Calhoon. Want to take it with you?

CALHOON: What?

DENTIST: Your tooth.

CALHOON: Tooth?

DENTIST: Your wisdom tooth.

CALHOON: Oh.

NURSE: It's good luck, sir.

CALHOON: *(Taking tooth.)* Thanks. Thank you.

(Calhoon examines tooth and sings as Dentist and Nurse resume security guard identities and positions.)

CALHOON: *Wisdom comes*
When wisdom wants
Glowing in the dark
Shining at the heart of me
Singing like the lark

I've left the shores of sorry
And sad is far behind
And just ahead lies Oolagong
Where folks is passing kind

MALE SECURITY GUARD: Want to pass your bag through, sir?

CALHOON: Excuse me?

MALE SECURITY GUARD: You coming through or what?

CALHOON: Indeed I am. *(Putting suitcase on baggage scanner.)* And thanks.

MALE SECURITY GUARD: For what?

(Calhoon passes through the body scanner.)

CALHOON: *(To female security guard.)* And how about you, darlin'? You got a hug for me? It's a terrible long flight home.
(Calhoon hugs female security guard, picks up suitcase and exits, whistling, as security guards resume positions. Lights fade to black.)

END OF PLAY

HAERE MAI
KI AOTEAROA
(Welcome to the Land
of the Long White Cloud)

by Julie McKee

To Paul

ORIGINAL PRODUCTION
Haere Mai Ki Aotearoa was directed by Jessica Bauman with the following cast:

Fiona . . . . .Amy Wright

PLAYWRIGHT'S BIOGRAPHY
Plays by Julie McKee in the HB series are *Invitation to a Funeral; Jill On a Recliner, Reading,* and *The Daffodils,* all published by Smith and Kraus. Other short plays include *A Backward Glance, The "Far-Flung,"* and *A Farewell to Mum* (EST Marathons and published by Smith and Kraus). Recent full-length plays include *Free Ascent, Get It While You Can,* and *The Adventures of Amy Bock* (Yale Repertory Theater, Sundance Playwrights Lab, Yale Summer Cabaret, HB Playwrights Foundation and a finalist in the Chesterfield Writer's Film Project). *A Play by Ear* is to be produced at the HB Playwrights Foundation in its 2001–02 season. Ms. McKee was commissioned by the Ensemble Studio Theatre/Alfred P. Sloan Foundation of Science and Technology Project to write *Fringe Benefits.* She is the recipient of the Truman Capote Fellowship and Eugene O'Neill Scholarship from Yale, and she recently received fellowships from the New York Foundation for the Arts, the MacDowell Colony, and Virginia Center for the Creative Arts. Ms. McKee is a graduate of the Yale School of Drama MFA Playwriting Program (1996).

CHARACTERS
      FIONA, fortyish. Has made a commitment to be optimistic. She has a dry
      sort of wit.

PLACE
      Customs area of an international airport in New Zealand.

TIME
      The present.

HAERE MAI KI AOTEAROA
(Welcome to the Land of the Long White Cloud)

As the lights come up, we see Fiona with three pieces of baggage, a carry-on bag, a duty-free bag, passport, customs and missing baggage forms in one hand, massaging her neck with the other.

FIONA: *(Reading a large Welcome to New Zealand banner, written in Maori, on the fourth wall. She is clearly agitated.)*
"Haere Mai ki Aotearoa." [Hi-ree my kee Ay-o-taya-ro-ah.]
Welcome to New Zealand?!
That will be the day. They've gone and lost my bloody bag, haven't they? Wankers. You pay all this money to fly from one side of the world to another, And what do they do? Not their job at any rate! What can I say? And of course my baggage claim tickets have disappeared. It's all just so terribly, terribly, terribly inconvenient.

I'm Fiona, Fee for short. Hi. Well I just got here, as you can see, and I'm just a bit fed up. All the other passengers have gone through, and I'm waiting here like a complete arsehole, pardon my French. I was just about to go through customs, with nothing to declare, when I realized, just in time, that I'm one bag short, and my family's out there, who I haven't laid eyes on in years and years, must be wondering what the hell is going on! Well that's New Zealand for you, "only third world country with running water," and I can't even have a smoke. Can I? No. All right. Well. It's an anticlimax is what it is.

Oh but lookee here. I do have a bottle of Johnny Walker Black Label, it's for my brother in law who has renal failure, cigarettes are for my sister who had breast cancer, a bottle of really good wine for myself, and GAP T-shirts for the nephews. Perhaps I could have a wee drink while I'm waiting, and if I could get the cork out of this bloody rotten bottle I would. *(She opens the bottle of Black Label instead and takes a swig.)*

Cheers. Oh yes. So — . Here I am back in the country where I was born, where my parents were born and their parents before them. I have returned to celebrate their fiftieth wedding anniversary and I have just left my husband.

(She takes another swig from the bottle.)

On the plane I dreamt I was still married. It's probably just the jet lag. It's four o'clock in the morning for me right now, yesterday. Twenty-two hours door to door. One more door to go. That one over there, red, to declare, or over there green, nothing to declare.

(Conspiratorially.) I haven't told them I've left him, not yet, I'm going to wait for the right moment, see how the land lies. I mainly want to connect. With them. My family. I want them to understand how I feel, that's all. And of course I want to know how they feel too.

(She stiffens in pain.)

There's something wrong with my neck. Can I sit on this I wonder? Will it bear my weight?

(She sits on her suitcase.)

"Be right back," she says, the girl behind the counter, "be right back." That must have been half an hour ago. We're on Kiwi time now, I'm back in the old country now.

I'm from here, of course. *New Zealand.* I know I don't sound like I'm from New Zealand, but I am. Most people think New Zealand is Australia and ask if we have kangaroos. We don't! We don't have snakes, aborigines, or koala bears either. New Zealand is 1,500 miles to the right of Australia, it's half way to Los Angeles from New York, which is where I live these days. In fact where I have lived for the last twenty years — And don't ask me how I ended up in New York, because it's a long story, in fact, it's another story. But! Because of recent events, like my divorce, I'm seriously thinking I have to, *absolutely have to, do something,* about changing my life. *(Pause.)* I don't know how though. Bit of a problem. Perhaps go back to school — I shouldn't say, "go back to school" because I never actually, really went to school to begin with — in the American sense, that is. I left school at sixteen without my school certificate, without my — what do you call it — my high school diploma, which is why I traveled early. I went everywhere when I was young. *(Joyously.)* Everywhere!

(Settling in.) You see, in my opinion the true traveler travels light, does not always know where she is going and does not wear a watch, time ceases to exist, she learns to savor the moment — she connects.

(Fiona massages her neck.)
I'm not myself, you see, and I've forgotten who I used to be, but they're sure to remind me sooner or later.
(Fiona glances at her watch.)
I'm also wearing a watch. One thing you have to remember though — God, you can't stand out — God forbid you should stand out. It's what we call "the tall poppy syndrome." Probably something to do with Flanders Fields, the First World War and the Anzacs — Australian and New Zealand Army Corps — in the trenches, "over the top we go," cannon fodder —

And I've just finished reading a book about ex-patriots and identity, you know, in preparation for this trip, and even though I have lived outside of my birth place for so long and have dual citizenship, I've begun to think of myself as a — as a — what you call a Pakeha [pah-kee-ha] New Zealander. "Pakeha being an indigenous expression to describe New Zealand people and things that are *not* Maori" [Mao-ree]. I'm not sure what this all means, but I'm pretty sure my family would disapprove. *(Whispering.)* They are slightly racist. But who isn't. I imagine they are waiting patiently or perhaps by now, impatiently, on the other side of that door, looking for someone they hope they recognize and complaining about how many brown faces there are, how many of them don't speak English, and counting the number of Asians. There are some things that do not change. One of them has a tendency to use the "N" word. Sends me into paroxysms of shame and indignation, but I don't dare say anything, do I? Once I did and was promptly told to mind my own bloody business. They do it to bait me, of course. But I've since learned not to take the bait! Well not that particular bait anyway.

I don't visit them often, well it's so far away, isn't it? Twenty-two hours door-to-door, and it's quite expensive. *(Very brightly.)* I am happy to be here though. Really happy. Thrilled in fact! Despite this ridiculous inconvenience.

People often ask me why I live there, and they live here, in their little house, half way across the other side of the world, but when you consider that *all of us* are "born into the second act of a tragedy" and that we spend the rest of our lives trying to make it into a comedy, or is it a romance, take your pick, it's hardly surprising, is it?

(Very brightly.) Anyway — the thing is, here I am! Back in New Zealand, one of the most beautiful places on earth — outside of Utah — I'll be staying in their little house for the big event, my parents fiftieth. Wedding anniversary. Tomorrow night they're having the party at their little house. We've all been looking forward to it for simply ages, and ages and. Ages.

If I know my mum, she'll be up at the crack of dawn, and down to the hairdressers, Dad'll be over at the off-license picking up the order of booze, and Noelene, my big sister, will be organizing everything else, and I mean everything else, and I'll attempt to give everyone a hand, which of course no-one needs because Mum and Noelene have had it all arranged since before I was born, and all of them think I'm useless in a kitchen anyway, which I am!

(Very brightly.) Still! It's not too late for an old dog to learn new tricks. As a matter of fact, I have just learned how to use a computer, Microsoft Word, so I temp. I'm a temp now. It's about the only thing I think I can do to make a living besides waitressing or bartending, either of which I just don't fancy to tell you the truth. I just don't think I'd get the tips and I have a bad back and I'm sure to end up with an equally bad attitude. *(She stiffens in pain.)* There seems to be something really wrong with my neck. *(Extremely brightly.)* But! I am beginning to set myself up very nicely for my new life. I've rented a furnished room with a separate bathroom, (I couldn't imagine sharing that with a stranger, dear God!) from an English professor on Central Park West, lovely man, lovely location, Upper West Side, sunny. I called all our friends to let them know where I was, and um. Funny thing was, none of them returned my calls. People took sides. They took his.

Sometimes I think how nice it would be to live here, in New Zealand. Aotearoa, the Land of the Long White Cloud. The prodigal daughter returns, except I don't know anyone here anymore, do I? Except them.

(She refers to her family through the doors.)
I've always fancied a home with a garden, a car, a sea view. A dog.

By tomorrow morning, if I ever get out of here, I should think I'll be having brunch with my sister, Noelene up at her house, which is just a couple of blocks away from my mother's house and. It's sure to be lovely. Too. And we'll be really, really nice and pleasant to each other, I imagine. We'll chat about how much this and that cost, and where to get the best cut of meat, and what night's the best night to go to the mall, and — ah . . . and . . . during the course of cutting up the vegetables for the party dip, I'll spring it on her then. That I've left my husband.

She is my only sister, only sibling in fact, and of course we don't see each other for years at a time and. I just want her to understand how I feel, and I want to know how she feels too. I mean how did she feel when her first husband left her? Not that my husband left me, it was the other way around, but I mean, my heart broke, really . . . I mean I still feel, *felt* . . . I felt terrible, guilty, God . . . I felt as if I'd let mum and dad down. Why should I feel that? I don't know why, but I do. *Did* . . . Did you know that a break up is as traumatic as a death, and I certainly felt as though a death had taken place, not to mention failure because my mother, bless her soul, told me that if I had a traditional wedding, which I did, it would be the proudest moment of her life. It was certainly the scariest moment of mine. Besides leaving him, that is.
(Pause.)
(Excited.) Oh look, oh look! You see those people over there. They're Maori! They're the indigenous people of New Zealand I was talking about before. I haven't seen any in quite a while. They look nice, don't they? They're not very prevalent in New York of course. Those ones over there, they're not Maori, even though they look like Maori. They're from the "Islands," though which islands I haven't a clue, probably the Cook Islands or Samoa. You can tell by the sarong. Maoris don't traditionally wear the sarong.

People always ask what it's like for the Maori, and did we do to them what they did to the Native American. I say, "No! No. No. Of course not. How could we? We were never that brutal." But in fact I have no idea what we did, or didn't do to them. I'm somewhat out of touch, you see. I really don't know what I'm talking about, except that the Maori are upset and so are the Pakeha, terribly, terribly, terribly upset with each other. It's a shame, a real shame!

(Fiona is by now terribly upset herself.)

I've filled out all the forms. Where is that girl from behind the counter? That young, bright, pretty, cheerful. And I have my whole life ahead of me! I also have a lot of invaluable experience, you've heard of that?

For example, I've been living in the United States for a number of years, I've been to Singapore. I've been to Bali. I've also traveled on the Marrakech Express, I've seen the Greek Islands, I've been to North Africa, Spain, Bahrain . . . "A wreck-on tour." But then I got travel burnout, which eventually turned into life burn out . . . andum andum . . . then I got married. Then I.

Oops. My eyes just went out of focus. *(She finds her way back to the suitcase and sits.)* All right, I'm all right now. And of course I've just been trained on the computer, so now I can work as a temporary secretary. Something I've always loathed and despised . . . but it beats being the female bathroom attendant in O'Grady's Pub on St. Patrick's Day. *(Pause.)* I cried that day. That was a low point that day. *(Determinedly optimistic.)* But! I have decided to be optimistic. At this stage, things can only go one way. I mean since I left my husband I've been renting a furnished room on Central Park West, from a really boring, pedantic man with bad breath, who never shuts up, but it's a nice neighborhood, until I get myself settled here, there, or school. No, no, no. No school. All that . . . (youth). And where the hell is she!!? Pollyanna with the paperwork!!?

(She looks around.)

Where did everyone go? I'm the only one here now. I wonder if they've. If they've forgotten me. Do you think they could have — *(Pause.)* Perhaps I should go and freshen up while I'm waiting. I'm feeling a bit. Sticky. My teeth feel a bit.

(She looks around for a ladies room.)

There's one over there. First appearances and all that, daughter flying in from New York and all that. Impress all the neighbors, relatives that everyone hates. Hope to God they recognize me. Ha, ha, ha, just joking. I sent a photo.

Wonder what they'd say if I told them I was taking antidepressants, not that it's anything to be ashamed of but they just wouldn't. I don't think they'd. So I won't. Ha, ha, ha. Bugger them!! I haven't even told them I left my husband! Oh God. But! I have made something up, you know, something I think *they* will understand, something that won't make me look bad. Like. For example. Children. I did, he didn't. That will work don't you think? I think so. Yeah. Christ.

I'm still telling them lies. I can't help it. It's like I'm a teenager again. Sneaking around. Then I left home, went overseas, stopped lying. I was just brutally truthful and to hell with the consequences. I think that's when I was a rebel, when I was free. When I was young. When I traveled. Traveled light. But since I decided to be a socially correct person, which was when I got married, I've never been able to tell them the truth. I told them I was happy, which made them happy and it made me one of them. As much as you can be one of them, when one of the them insists on using the "N" word just to get a rise out of you.

But no matter how far away you live from each other, that umbilical cord will reach, will find you no matter whether you're traveling light or not. It's like a goddamned homing device!!

I don't know. Perhaps it's just not possible to tell the truth to one's family. The whole truth.

Surely there must be more important things to lie about in this big wide world than.

I married my husband because he was the kindest man I ever knew. Getting married was the scariest, most touching, and most sacred thing I have ever done.

I haven't told you why I left my husband, have I?

Well I wonder where my bag is. Do you know I can't even remember what's in it. *(Long pause.)* Did I even bring it? Oh. *(Beat.)* Oh. Don't say that. One, two, three . . . Was there a fourth? *(Beat.)* Oh God. You know I can't. I can't. Remember. *(Pause.)* And I've reported it, I've made a big fuss over it, I threatened to tear the place apart with my! Oh God — and there's the girl! Is it her? Yes! Here she comes.

Oh I think I better. Do I have time? Oh God. I think I'll just. Where did I see?

(She looks around for the ladies room.)

Oh there. Till she's out of sight. How embarrassing, how very, very, very . . .

(Fiona stops in her tracks.)

Christ! It's all right, it's all right, Fiona!

(Fiona stands her ground, and to the young woman approaching . . .)

It's all right! I've found it!

(Fiona considers what she has just said.)

I've found it? Oops. No.

(Back to the girl.)

Oops! Not a problem. No, not a problem!

(Fiona rips up the missing bag form.)

Yes?

(Pause, then back to the audience.)

Yes. That was unfortunate. That was very, very. *(Beat.)* Never mind. I'm all right, I'm all right now and. All in one piece? *(Pause.)* Yes. So.

(She gathers a couple of bags.)

(Embarrassed.) Oh ah. About New Zealand being a third world country with. Running water. I didn't mean it. Not really.

(Fiona gathers the rest of her bags then . . .)

Here we go. Nothing to declare.

(She walks to the green door, then stops.)

Here we go.

(She walks determinedly through the green door — the nothing-to-declare door.)

END OF PLAY

WHERE I COME FROM

by Daniel Reitz

*I would like to thank the Yaddo Corporation,
where this play was written.
It is dedicated to Brian Keane.*

ORIGINAL PRODUCTION

Where I Come From was directed by Jules Ochoa with the following cast:

Mark . . . . Grant Goodman
Shay . . . . Ryan Dunn
Aziz . . . . Jason Madera

PLAYWRIGHT'S BIOGRAPHY

Daniel Reitz's plays have been developed and produced at numerous theaters, including the Mark Taper Forum, the Joseph Papp Public Theater, Naked Angels, Manhattan Class Company, Playwrights Horizons, Ensemble Studio Theatre, and Circle Repertory. He was a recipient of a 2000 fellowship from The New York Foundation for the Arts, a Drama-Logue Award, and *L.A. Weekly* Theater Critics and Ovation Award nominations. For his play *Where I Come From,* he was a finalist for the Heideman Award at the Actors Theatre of Louisville's Humana Festival. He has also received writing fellowships from the Edward Albee Foundation, the MacDowell Colony, the Virginia Center for the Creative Arts, the Yaddo Corporation, and the Hawthornden Castle International Retreat for Writers in Scotland.

Urbania, his screenplay adaptation of his play *Urban Folk Tales,* was voted Best Film at film festivals in Los Angeles, San Francisco, Philadelphia, and Provincetown, was nominated for a Grand Jury Prize at the Sundance Film Festival, and was an official selection of the Toronto and Seattle film festivals before its release by Lions Gate Films in 2000. The film also received a GLAAD Media Award nomination. He adapted his play *Regular Joe* as a short film and wrote and directed the short *Height of Cool,* both of which have been screened at film festivals in the United States and Europe.

As an occasional journalist, he has written for the *New York Times* and *Salon.*

CHARACTERS

MARK, thirties.
SHAY, late twenties.
AZIZ, thirties.

PLACE

A passenger terminal at John F. Kennedy International Airport.

WHERE I COME FROM

In the passenger waiting area of Kennedy Airport, Shay and Mark sit together against the wall, by themselves. Shay looks through a travel guidebook. Mark flips through the pages of a men's health and fitness magazine. Aziz sits nearby, by himself, his face hidden behind an Arabic-language newspaper.

MARK: We're really early. Practically no one here.

SHAY: How early are we? We're only —

MARK: Five hours. Early.

SHAY: Better to be early —

MARK: Than late? *(He looks over at Aziz, reading his newspaper.)* One other guy and us.

(She looks up from her guidebook, smiling at him.)

SHAY: Ships of the desert. *(She prods him.)* Camels. I told you this, right? You can actually buy one. I mean, you can rent but you can also buy.

MARK: Camel co-op.

SHAY: For as little as 600 U.S. dollars.

MARK: If I buy one, I want to take it home. I buy, it's mine, baby.

SHAY: I'm sure it's been done. *(She goes back to her book.)* "Take care when riding however — " . . . hmm ". . . that you have many soft layers to sit on, otherwise your thighs and bottom might be an oozing mass of sores."

MARK: Oozing mass. That paints a picture. How about a rent-a-car?

SHAY: We're gonna go there and not ride a camel?

MARK: I'd get by. But I'm sure you'll see to it that I'll be on one.

SHAY: When you see me way up there, you'll just be dyin' to be right up there with me. *(She peruses her book.)* Public toilets sound a little scary . . . squat-over-hole-types for the most part. Well, Paris is also like that.

MARK: Paris? Where in Paris is it like that?

SHAY: Remember that Middle Eastern café? *(Reads.)* "Only in the finer hotels will toilet paper be available."

MARK: What do they do?

(She silently reads, then looks at him.)

SHAY: Water squirter. *(She continues to peruse her book.)* Here's something interesting, how'd I miss this? You bring in your laundry to these little laundry places . . . where they have these guys called *muk*wagees . . . muk*wa*gees? . . . ironing men . . . who take these old old ancient irons which open at the top and which they fill with hot coals . . . then they fill their mouths with water and . . . huh . . . they spray the water from their mouths onto the clothes as they iron.

(Aziz, hearing this, lowers his newspaper and steals a look at Shay, then lifts his newspaper back up to his face.)

SHAY: *(Continues.)* At this point I should probably review the safety tips for women travelers.

MARK: Again? It's like you're preparing for something to happen.

SHAY: Better safe than sorry.

MARK: Why go at all?

SHAY: *(Smiles.)* I'm not afraid.

MARK: Intrepid girl scout. I think you dig the idea.

SHAY: What idea?

MARK: Danger.

SHAY: *(Laughs.)* There's no danger. If I wanted danger, believe me, there are places to go for that. No, this is junior high stuff. *(Reads.)* "Wear a wedding ring . . . more respect for a woman who's married . . . if traveling with a man, it's better to say you're married even if you're not."

MARK: Okay. So we will.

SHAY: What if I don't want to?

MARK: That's your choice. But don't look to me to protect you.

(She looks at him, then looks back to her book.)

I'm kidding. Right? You know that?

SHAY: Do I? Maybe I should test you. Put myself in some kind of danger.

MARK: I thought it was junior high stuff.

SHAY: I could find some somewhere. See what you're made of.

MARK: I'm tougher than I look. I just keep a low profile, that's all.

SHAY: I know. I've seen you enraged before.

MARK: Just don't get my dander up. Then the fur will fly.

(She smiles, kissing him.)

You don't want that.

SHAY: *(Reads.)* "Avoid direct eye contact with men — wear dark sunglasses. Be careful when camel riding . . . not unusual for a man to ride up alongside and grab a woman. Riding ahead of a man on a camel is basically inviting harassment . . . you might want to memorize the Arabic for "don't touch me.""

MARK: See, maybe we should skip the camels.

SHAY: *Gamal.* Camel is *gamal.*

MARK: Maybe we should skip the *gamals.*

SHAY: Not with you there to protect me.

MARK: Oh, yeah, I forgot.

SHAY: *(Reads.)* "The idea that any Western woman is more than willing to jump into bed with any Middle Eastern man has given many of these men the notion that Western women are there solely for their pleasure. Being grabbed or rubbed up against is often considered completely acceptable behavior . . . reports of men exposing themselves or *even masturbating are not unusual.*"

MARK: Sshh!

SHAY: I'm just telling you what it says.

MARK: Yeah, well, do you have to emphasize certain sections?

SHAY: That's not worth emphasizing?

MARK: Why don't you focus on something a little more mundane — like the current exchange rate. *(He looks over at Aziz.)* Or read quieter.

SHAY: *La tilmasni!*

(Aziz looks up again from his newspaper. Mark looks at her.)

SHAY: "Don't touch me." *(Pause. She flips pages.)* Blah blah blah. *(Reads.)* "Exercise caution when taking pictures . . . it is forbidden to photograph airports, bridges, train stations, military areas . . ."

(Mark takes out his camera.)

MARK: Shit.

SHAY: What?

MARK: I never got a new battery for the camera.

SHAY: We can't get one there?

MARK: You wanna risk it? No, I saw a shop back there. I'm going.

(Mark exits. Pause. Aziz lowers his newspaper.)

AZIZ: Interesting.

(She takes no notice of him.)

AZIZ: Fascinating, actually.

(She looks at him.)

SHAY: Excuse me?

AZIZ: I said fascinating.

SHAY: Is it. What is.

AZIZ: I heard a bit of your exchange just now with your . . . husband. Toilets and such. Americans. Always surprised and chagrined to discover discomfort awaiting them. But really it should be embraced in exchange for the rewards acquired.

(Pause.)

SHAY: Actually, he isn't my husband. And if we're talking about toilets and such . . . if you mean putting up with a little . . . I mean, I hate to use the word "primitive" because that sounds negative and elitist in that tiresome Western way, but if you mean enduring conditions we're not used to enduring in order just to be there and experience all the glories that a place has to off —

AZIZ: Perhaps that is what I mean.

SHAY: Perhaps? *(Pause.)* Then I agree with you. But I have to say I didn't really like the way you said Americans.

AZIZ: Excuse me. Westerners.

SHAY: It's just . . . no, it's just, it's how you said it. "Americans."

AZIZ: It's merely a word. Or perhaps you mean my inflection?

SHAY: A word is merely a word. Americans are people. Not that I'm some patriot or anything, just . . .

AZIZ: Certainly. People. But merely people. With the usual inner organs. Livers, spleens, hearts, and blood that flows around all of these. That has flowed and will flow.

(Mark returns, the camera around his neck, holding a can of coke, a bag, and a magazine. Aziz watches him as he sits down. Shay watches Aziz watching Mark. Silence. Mark looks up.)

MARK: Fuck me.

SHAY: What.

MARK: Jesus Christ. I forgot the goddamn battery. I got everything but, I get magazines and gum and . . . shit.

(He gets up, tosses the magazine down on his seat, exits.)

AZIZ: That is not your husband. That's good.

(Pause.)

SHAY: Is it. Why?

(He waves his hand dismissively.)

Look. You started this conversation.

AZIZ: No, I believe you did. You were speaking, I felt, to be heard. That's unusual where I come from.

SHAY: Where is that?

AZIZ: Where you are going.

(Pause.)

SHAY: I don't think I was speaking to be heard. I certainly haven't solicited your opinion on the person I'm with.

AZIZ: Person. Yes.

SHAY: Man.

AZIZ: Not your husband. *(Pause.)* You were speaking of my country. You were speaking of the men in my country. You were speaking of me.

SHAY: Was I?

AZIZ: You didn't know you were?

   (Pause.)

SHAY: I didn't notice you.

AZIZ: Ah. My mistake.

   (Pause.)

SHAY: But I notice you now.

AZIZ: In that case, I am Aziz. Pleasure.

SHAY: Shay. The man who is not my husband is named Mark. Why did you say that earlier?

AZIZ: Remind me.

SHAY: "Merely people"?

AZIZ: Only Americans think the idea of humanity — should I say their humanity? — is unique.

SHAY: Fine, I'll go along with that. But you said something else. Something about blood.

AZIZ: (Smiles.) I have a habit, a danger or an amusement, depending on what country I am in. I might say certain words, Americans, blood, two words in the same sentence, perhaps they mean nothing, merely words. "Words, words, words," as that wise Westerner Shakespeare wrote.

SHAY: But they might not.

AZIZ: Precisely. I may say things like "Allah's will be done." Words that are beautiful to some are ominous to the ears of others. But you see that words sometimes are mere words with no portent. Example: I might say, "What's done cannot be undone." From my mouth to your ears. I am merely quoting *Macbeth*. Or am I?

SHAY: Or maybe you're just trying to scare me.

   (Pause.)

AZIZ: Perhaps you know if I act out it's because I am doing so to satisfy your expectations of me. (He stands.) But I heartily agree with your little book on one point. (He walks over to her.) Be very careful of just who you ride your camel in front of.

   (Standing directly in front of Shay, Aziz unzips his pants, exposes himself to her, zips up, moves away, and sits back down. He resumes reading his newspaper. Silence. Mark re-enters. He sits down, removes the camera battery from its package, inserts it into the camera. He looks at Shay through the camera, then lowers the camera, and looks directly at her.)

MARK: What's the matter?

SHAY: What do you mean?

MARK: I mean you look funny.

SHAY: Actually, I have a headache. Can you go get me some aspirin?

MARK: Are you kidding me?

SHAY: Yes, I'm kidding. Why would I kid about a headache? I have a headache.

MARK: You want me to go back all the way to where I just came to buy you aspirin?

SHAY: No, I expect nothing from you.

(Pause.)

MARK: You don't have any on you?

SHAY: If I did, would I ask you to get me some? Look, if you're just gonna whine about it —

MARK: Fine, fine, don't . . . I'll get you aspirin.

(He exits.)

AZIZ: Mark. If I said he is an easy mark, again, mere words. In my case, "easy mark" is the phrase, I believe?

(Mark returns, flushed with frustration.)

SHAY: *(To Mark, angrily.)* What?

MARK: What? I'll tell ya, I'm outta fuckin' money, that's what. I bought two magazines and a coke and gum and a candy bar and a camera battery, it cost me nineteen bucks, all I had was a twenty.

SHAY: That was all the cash you had on you?

MARK: Ya want a breakdown, Okay . . . the car service, the Starbucks. *(He shows her the inside of his wallet.)* A bunch of fifty-dollar traveler's checks and ten thousand *irsh.* You want your aspirin gimme some scratch.

(She unzips her backpack, takes out her wallet, and thrusts money into Mark's hand. He stalks off.)

AZIZ: Once again, we are alone.

SHAY: I could have your hairy ass arrested for that little stunt.

AZIZ: Not where I'm from. And forgive me for saying but it's slightly offensive to suggest that because I'm a man of Middle Eastern origin my, as you say, ass must therefore be hairy. That kind of logic might too suggest that perhaps I'm, as you also say, hung —

SHAY: I would never say that.

AZIZ: Like a *gamal.* At any rate I've no doubt that mine is bigger than his.

SHAY: Since I'm the only one who knows definitively, then only I can say.

AZIZ: I understand why you are not married to that.

SHAY: You understand nothing.

AZIZ: Perhaps. Perhaps not.

SHAY: He's my lover.

AZIZ: With such a little thing between his legs? *(Pause.)* No. He won't marry you. *(Pause.)* I wouldn't marry you, either.

SHAY: No, you're just content to expose yourself to me. A stranger.

AZIZ: Not a stranger. A woman.

(He smiles. He takes out a cigarette.)

SHAY: There is no smoking section here.

AZIZ: *(Laughs.)* Smoking section. Nonsmoking section. Very American. *(Pause.)* I am only fulfilling your dream of me. *(Pause.)* You sent him away to be alone with me. *(Silence.)*

(Shay stares at Aziz. She smiles. She laughs. She throws her hair back, shakes her head. She stands, slowly walking over to him.)

SHAY: You don't see much female hair hanging like this. Do you?

(She gathers her hair to one side and moves behind him.)

The guidebook says it's often a good idea to wear a scarf over your hair. *(She drops her hair over his face. He reaches up and touches her hair lightly. She flings her hair back.)*

Could you smell the guava . . . the ginger . . . the herbal essences? *(She moves her arms down the front of him, lifting up his shirt. With one hand she reaches underneath the shirt, feeling his chest.)*

The guidebook says . . . be very careful not to behave in a way that might be considered flirtatious or . . . salacious . . .or suggestive. You might be in for no end of trouble.

(Pause.)

Mmnn. I'm thinking of those mukwagees . . . filling their mouths with water . . . spitting it onto the underwear of American women with all the contempt they can muster.

(She puts two fingers in his mouth.)

You'd spit on my lingerie if given the chance, wouldn't you? You dirty mukwagee.

(She removes her fingers from his mouth and wipes them on his shirt.)

Perhaps you know if I act out it's because I am doing so to satisfy your expectations of me.

(She moves away from him and sits down. She opens her guidebook and reads. Silence. Mark enters.)

MARK: Here. *(He holds up a tin of aspirin.)* First say I don't whine.

SHAY: You don't.

(He tosses her the tin of aspirin and sits down. She turns to him, draping her leg over his. Smiles.)

SHAY: Thanks.

(He nods. She strokes his head.)

MARK: Pisses me off when you say that. I'm not nine and don't whine.

(She kisses him, as Aziz watches.)

MARK: If you're nice and behave yourself . . . and don't say I whine again . . . maybe I'll ride a fucking *gamal*. Maybe.

(She kisses him again. Silence. Aziz stands. He addresses them.)

AZIZ: Arrival in a place is always something to be thankful for. There is a phrase, and you might well hear it around you — the relief of fellow travelers as they murmur *illHamdu lillah 'as-salaama* — "Thank God we have arrived safely." Then again, you might well not hear that. Depending on how the journey goes. *(Aziz extends his hand to Mark. They shake hands.)* I wish us all a good journey, eh, Mark? Now, I must go and relieve myself in a Western toilet. *(Aziz takes Shay's hand, kisses it, and strolls off, snapping open and shut his lighter as he exits.)*

MARK: Who the fuck was that?

SHAY: That . . . was Aziz.

(Blackout.)

END OF PLAY

TERMINAL CONNECTION

by Ari Roth

Terminal Connection originally appeared in the 1999 HB Playwrights Foundation Airport Play Festival; directed by Jim Milton with the following cast:

Morgan .... Peter Birkenhead
Cordelia .... Paula Gruskiewicz

PLAYWRIGHT'S BIOGRAPHY

Ari Roth is the author of *Born Guilty,* based on the book of interviews by Peter Sichrovsky, originally commissioned and produced by Arena Stage, off-Broadway at the American Jewish Theater, and over thirty other productions across the country. Most recently, it was produced in repertory with its sequel, *Peter and the Wolf,* commissioned by the National Foundation for Jewish Culture (NFJC). *Goodnight Irene* was commissioned by Manhattan Theatre Club with a grant from the NFJC and has been produced at the Performance Network in Ann Arbor, Hypothetical Theatre Company in New York, and at Theater J in Washington, D.C., where Mr. Roth serves as artistic director. His play *Life in Refusal,* produced at Theater J in 2000, was nominated for a Charles MacArthur/Helen Hayes Award for Outstanding New Play (as was *Born Guilty* in 1992). His comedy, *Oh, The Innocents,* won the Clifford Davy Award for its production at GeVa Theater, directed by Joe Mantello. It was subsequently produced at HB Playwrights Foundation, directed by Artistic Director William Carden. *Love and Yearning in the Not-For-Profits and Other Marital Distractions* premiered at Theater J in spring 2001 and was originally workshopped at the Ojai Playwrights Conference. The play is expanded from one-acts originally produced at HB Playwrights Foundation. Mr. Roth is a recipient of a National Endowment for the Arts Workshop Grant nominated by Northlight Theatre and has had his one-acts produced at Ensemble Studio Theater, Circle Rep, and the Double Image Short Play Festival. He is a graduate of the University of Michigan where he won two Hopwood Awards for playwriting, and has taught at the University of Michigan, Brandeis, and New York University.

TERMINAL CONNECTION

Lights up on Cordelia, late thirties, deplaning. She looks behind her — Is he coming? Looks up. At the dome. And then behind. And then up. As a man emerges from the jet-way. Cordelia starts rummaging through her shoulder bag; she finds a notepad. The man is dressed in a suit.

MORGAN: You waited.

CORDELIA: Oh . . . No, I was just, uhm . . . Hi . . . taking note. Of the terminal. "Marine Terminal." An airport with actual portholes.

MORGAN: Are there? I don't see . . .

CORDELIA: Suggested. Suggested portholes. And if not? Well then, hell, there should be!

MORGAN: With a name like "Marine Terminal!"

(They share a forced laugh. He is ready to walk.)

So? Are you . . . ?

CORDELIA: I often make notes; to myself. To remind myself. If I want to remember; a moment; an insight; a flash of intuition.

MORGAN: Go on . . .

CORDELIA: I can't remember what it was! No, wait! Ah! "The airport as convergent space. Hub where all destinations appear possible, except the planetary and the stationary . . .

(Stepping forward, to audience.)

And runways beckon in all directions; all away from where one is supposed to be; where one has *agreed* to be, come dinner, which is now; which is home; where one isn't. One is here; with "a person"; a person who was a stranger who now is more, and so one really must be going.

MORGAN: You know, I really enjoyed our conversation . . .

CORDELIA: Yes, I . . . So did —

MORGAN: I hope you don't think I was being —

CORDELIA: No!

MORGAN: Overly . . .

CORDELIA: *God,* no! I hope you don't think *I* was being —

MORGAN: Not at all!

CORDELIA: Because I'm glad we talked.

MORGAN: Or *whatever it is* that we . . .

CORDELIA: Wept. I believe that we wept.

MORGAN: And how is that possible, by the way? When I never weep. Or cry,
for that matter. Especially not on a half-hour shuttle.

CORDELIA: Well, couple a First Class Mimosas will do the trick!

MORGAN: Thank God for wind shears!

CORDELIA: Thank God for wind shears! My God. Is that why we were circling?
I wasn't paying attention. To the captain.

MORGAN: "Wind shears in the vicinity." They were reported. I think so.

CORDELIA: We could have fallen out of the sky!

MORGAN: That I don't think.

CORDELIA: You don't?

MORGAN: *(Ready to go.)* So . . . ?

CORDELIA: I barely either — Cry. Or weep, for that matter. Or do much of
anything in First Class! I was today because of my upgrades. We get them
from the Cultural Alliance.

MORGAN: How enlightened of the Cultural Alliance. To give upgrades to peo-
ple who might actually *appreciate* . . .
(Another forced laugh.)
So did you say which way you were — ?

CORDELIA: I hate short flights. I like to settle in. For the long haul. To really
get somewhere. Like through a book.

MORGAN: And I kept you from reading.

CORDELIA: No.

MORGAN: With my questions.

CORDELIA: I liked your questions.

MORGAN: I can be that way. A terrier. I have heard this. People have said this
behind my back. Worse. To my face. That I can be a bulldog or a terrier.

CORDELIA: Not a nice range of choices.

MORGAN: I know.

CORDELIA: "Either way you're a dog."

MORGAN: I have heard that said too. Because I won't let go. To a line of ques-
tioning. Or professional pursuit. I've been accused of being too singu-
larly driven. Too Typically Male.

CORDELIA: I find the word "typical" to be a lazy word. I don't think you should
pay attention to —

MORGAN: What they mean is . . . What these people . . . my wife . . . . Well,
my ex — For all intents-and-purposes, "ex." What she means, I think, is
that I can be too narrowly focused and miss out on things.

CORDELIA: . . . You wouldn't happen to have a quarter?

MORGAN: Would you like my cell?

CORDELIA: It's just home. And I'm not really comfortable with cells.

MORGAN: And home is . . . ?

CORDELIA: I'm sorry?

MORGAN: Home. Is . . . ?

CORDELIA: Upper West Side. Moving someday! But for now it's . . . *(Finds one.)* Ah, a quarter.

MORGAN: I meant the "who" part. Not "where." But —

CORDELIA: My family.

MORGAN: You live with your family.

CORDELIA: Well, not my parents. I mean, that would be wonderful. But impossible.

MORGAN: Yes, you mentioned. Before. So you live with — ?

CORDELIA: My *husband.* I live with my *daughter.*

MORGAN: Which is wonderful.

CORDELIA: I should call them.

MORGAN: And this could be wonderful too, that's all I'm saying. To continue. A conversation. If you're up for continuing . . .? If you wanted to —

CORDELIA: Yes?

MORGAN: Y'know . . . Have dinner.

CORDELIA: I'm supposed to be *home* for dinner.

MORGAN: Or a drink. Or a ride. If you wanted a ride. I have a driver.

CORDELIA: You have a driver?

MORGAN: Luis. He's at baggage claim. Do you have any?

CORDELIA: Baggage?

MORGAN: That's where we meet. When I travel.

CORDELIA: You must travel a lot.

MORGAN: Always have. Wish I didn't. And you know what? I don't. But I do. I should stop.

CORDELIA: I should call.

MORGAN: Why don't we call from the car? It's a Town Car.

CORDELIA: A Town Car?

MORGAN: I could be sixty, I know! I used to drive an Infiniti. I don't be*lieve* in Infinity anymore. Now I believe in the power of Life and Death.

CORDELIA: Yes.

MORGAN: We are here, we are —

CORDELIA: Gone.

MORGAN: There is birth. There is —

CORDELIA: "Decay." You were saying —

MORGAN: And in the time of your life —

CORDELIA: Live!

MORGAN: Give! Give to others. And leave nothing behind. This I have learned. Only recently. Take the cell. Come on. It's free. I get a thousand free minutes.

CORDELIA: That's a lot.

MORGAN: I'm used to a lot. I'm thinking I should get used to a lot less. "Addition by subtraction"; that's what the sportscasters say. I haven't found that to be the case up to now.

CORDELIA: No, you mentioned.

MORGAN: But it's a road. Process of divestiture. Releasing oneself from one's things.

CORDELIA: I prefer more. "When in doubt, add." That's my motto. Addition by addition.

CORDELIA: Basic math.

MORGAN: So, here. The cell is here. The cell is free. Basic math. Check in. Phone home. And then we can . . .

CORDELIA: Yes?

MORGAN: Do whatever.

CORDELIA: *(Takes phone; out.)* "Do whatever?" What to do? Phone home and do what? Lie? How does one learn to lie, when one generally doesn't? *Ah . . . Practice-practice . . .*

MORGAN: Just press "Send" after you punch in the number.

CORDELIA: Right. Uhm. And where does the mouth go? I mean . . . Where do I put my . . . ?

MORGAN: You've never used a cell before?

CORDELIA: Oh, I've used a cell! I just try not to make a *habit* of . . . y'know, using . . . *strange* cells. Phone home.

MORGAN: Phone home.

(She dials. He sits.)

So you're not interested in caviar? Or oysters?

CORDELIA: No, that's . . .

MORGAN: Or a drink? Or a ride? Or, you mentioned you worked as a curator.

CORDELIA: *(Puts down the phone.)* I did?

MORGAN: Or maybe I just noticed the invitation. In your book. To an opening. A gallery showing. So you're the director *of . . .* ?

CORDELIA: A small one. Yes.

MORGAN: And I, of course, have a company. Also small. But nonetheless, in need of an overhaul. A redesign. Top-to-bottom. It's in midtown. Would you be interested in . . . ?

CORDELIA: In . . .

MORGAN: Tell you what. Check in. Phone home. Then we'll talk.

CORDELIA: No, what? I'm interested.

(She joins him. Opening her planner.)

You were saying? That you have . . . ?

MORGAN: A boardroom. That can't stay the way it is.

CORDELIA: And why is that?

MORGAN: Because it can't.

CORDELIA: But why?

MORGAN: Why don't we take a look at it? We can go right now if —

CORDELIA: I'm fine just staying here . . . If you want to talk about — ?

MORGAN: Why don't we talk about me hiring you?

CORDELIA: As . . . ?

MORGAN: A consultant. To come in. Reassess. Redesign. Top-to-bottom.

CORDELIA: That's a lot of . . .

MORGAN: Work? Indeed. For which, of course, I would pay. Many people. Not *just* you.

CORDELIA: No, I know —

MORGAN: I would pay for your training; your taste; your experience. You *do* have training and taste and experience?

CORDELIA: Up to a point.

MORGAN: And that point would be. . . ?

CORDELIA: Curating. I have experience with curating. In the not-for-profits.

MORGAN: And the difference between curating "in the not-for-profits" and consulting would be . . . ?

CORDELIA: Well, *Charging,* for one. We're not very good at it. I wouldn't know what to! I wouldn't know a ballpark!

MORGAN: How 'bout $10,000?

CORDELIA: I'm sorry.

MORGAN: How 'bout $10,000? As a ballpark. A recommendation. You to me. Tonight.

CORDELIA: $10,000?

MORGAN: Or any other night. It doesn't have to be tonight. If tonight scares you.

CORDELIA: It doesn't scare me.

MORGAN: So we're resolved about the ambiguity? Over what to charge?

CORDELIA: Uhm. $10,000 does seem like an awful lot —

MORGAN: You don't think you're worth it?

CORDELIA: I don't think that's the point.

MORGAN: Because I happen to *have* a ballpark. Idea. About consultants. I *have* experience, you see. I'm used to paying for things.

CORDELIA: One gets the impression.

MORGAN: It's what businesses do.

CORDELIA: I'm not a business.

MORGAN: You're in the art business.

CORDELIA: Such as it is.

MORGAN: So then it's yours to decide. What kind of business do you wish to be.

CORDELIA: Well. Maybe I'd just do it.

MORGAN: Do?

CORDELIA: Con*sult!* For free! Without making it quite so . . . Without money changing hands. Or pockets. Or . . .

MORGAN: And what would the advantage of that be? For you? I can see for me, but —

CORDELIA: Well, it might make it less of . . .

MORGAN: Yes?

CORDELIA: It could definitely make it feel less of . . .

MORGAN: Of?

CORDELIA: Of . . . You know.

MORGAN: No, I don't. Of . . . ?

CORDELIA: Of.. . Of a pick up.

MORGAN: Of a . . . ?

CORDELIA: Of a very expensive; yes . . .

MORGAN: I didn't mean for . . .

CORDELIA: Well, it does have the trappings. Of some movie? With Demi Moore? I mean, $10,000 for a dinner, plus —

MORGAN: Forget dinner.

CORDELIA: It's not the dinner! I don't want dinner! I don't want money! I don't want to be *paid.* I don't *need* to be.

MORGAN: Got it. A mistake. *My* mistake. You're very right. I'll go.

CORDELIA: Maybe that's . . .

MORGAN: We'll do it different. A more clear separation.

CORDELIA: I agree.

MORGAN: Here's my card. Give a call. Bring by the portfolio any . . .

CORDELIA: I didn't mean —

MORGAN: No, I think you did. You paint a graphic . . .

CORDELIA: I didn't mean to impugn . . .

MORGAN: I think you did mean . . . Something. And you're right. I'll put my money away.

CORDELIA: But I don't have a problem with your —

MORGAN: *(Sharp.)* Then why are you still standing here? Why are we even talking? *(A beat.)*

CORDELIA: It wasn't you. It was me. *I* was the one. *I* was the one. Picking *you* up? On the plane? I mean, the two of us. Sitting there. Each reading. To ourselves. Me *sniffling*.

MORGAN: Unintentionally.

CORDELIA: Yes, but audibly. You asking me *why*. Me *telling* you.

MORGAN: You *needing* to.

CORDELIA: Me *confiding* in you.

MORGAN: Me confiding in *you*.

CORDELIA: I shouldn't have sniffled.

MORGAN: I'm glad you did. Because otherwise I wouldn't have asked . . .

CORDELIA: "What's wrong?"

MORGAN: That's right.

CORDELIA: "I don't *know* what's wrong!"

MORGAN: Maybe nothing. Maybe it's just good to sniffle, when you're reading a really sad book.

CORDELIA: It wasn't the book.

MORGAN: I know it wasn't.

CORDELIA: *(After a beat.)* . . . I'll take a cab.

MORGAN: Let me give you a ride.

CORDELIA: No, that's . . .

MORGAN: I'd like to. I'd like to see where you live.

CORDELIA: It's nothing. Really. It's just . . .

MORGAN: You deserve better than nothing.

CORDELIA: No, I know. It's a rental, is what I . . .

MORGAN: You deserve wonderful. You seem wonderful. You seem to have wonderful taste.

CORDELIA: I . . .

MORGAN: A wonderful eye. For contrast. For conflict. And beauty. Coexisting. In the same frame.

CORDELIA: You can tell all that?

MORGAN: I was hoping I might *benefit* from it. And that you might as well.

CORDELIA: I —

MORGAN: Handsomely.

CORDELIA: *(Beat.)* . . . I'm not ashamed. That I opened up. Before. On the plane.

MORGAN: You shouldn't be.

CORDELIA: I was ripe to. I was just coming from . . .

MORGAN: Yes, you were —

CORDELIA: A very moving . . .

MORGAN: From a funeral.

CORDELIA: Such a beautiful funeral —

MORGAN: "A perfect day"; you were saying.

CORDELIA: Which are always the most difficult.

> *(Shorter pause.)*

MORGAN: . . . Actually, I would think *all* funerals are equally [difficult] —

CORDELIA: *(Before "difficult.")* No, that's right.

MORGAN: Memory tells me . . .

CORDELIA: No, you're right. They all are. But the contrast between the two . . .
With the weather, on the one hand; and then the mood . . . So fraught
. . . The breeze so light. It blew it all away. You could feel it. We all did.

MORGAN: Perfect strangers.

CORDELIA: I knew no one there.

MORGAN: Except your friend.

CORDELIA: Except for Sharon.

MORGAN: Your designer.

CORDELIA: *Former* designer —

MORGAN: And you left feeling connected —

CORDELIA: By memory.

MORGAN: To his memory.

CORDELIA: I didn't *have* a memory; of him. I had a memory of Sharon. *With*
him. *Worrying* about him. Worrying about a husband. And then I had a
memory of me . . .

MORGAN: Worrying about . . .

CORDELIA: Someone else.

MORGAN: Your mother. You said. It triggered.

CORDELIA: It must've. For everyone.

MORGAN: There was a feeling of congregation.

CORDELIA: A different memory in everyone.

MORGAN: Perfect strangers.

CORDELIA: A oneness with all things. Earth. Wind. Sky. Birds. Voices. Children's voices.

MORGAN: It's no wonder you were crying.

CORDELIA: But I had no right to make you.

MORGAN: How could you know?

CORDELIA: I didn't. I can't even imagine. That kind of loss.

MORGAN: I think you can. I think you have.

CORDELIA: But a child?

MORGAN: Loss is loss.

CORDELIA: And is devastating . . . How old?

MORGAN: Does it matter? I don't know that it does.

CORDELIA: But a baby? It was a baby, you said.

MORGAN: Loss is loss. And sickness sickness. And each is equally devastating. And destructive. And also a blessing. A signal. That "change is inevitable." And that clinging to anything . . .

CORDELIA: Is useless . . . ?

MORGAN: I'm more generous now than I ever was when my son . . . when my . . . when he . . . when . . .

CORDELIA: Damon . . .

MORGAN: Was alive.

CORDELIA: But you're alone. How is that? With all you've learned? What you talked about?

MORGAN: It's *all* talk. Or is the question, "Where's my *wife?*"

CORDELIA: No. I . . .

MORGAN: She's home. It isn't *my* home. But *she* is.

CORDELIA: And you are?

MORGAN: Stranded. In a terminal. Maybe suspended's the better word.

CORDELIA: I don't know where I'm supposed to be.

MORGAN: You should be where you want to be.

CORDELIA: *(Extending a hand.)* Cordelia. It's Cordelia.

MORGAN: It's Morgan.

CORDELIA: Hello, Morgan.

MORGAN: Where do you want to be, Cordelia?

CORDELIA: I'm supposed to be home for dinner.

MORGAN: You should have dinner. Where you want to; not just where you're supposed to.

CORDELIA: I'm familiar with the philosophy.

MORGAN: So where would you want to, if you wanted to; have dinner; with me, I mean?

CORDELIA: I don't want to go to midtown. I don't want to see your board-room. I don't want to go home. I want to stay. Right here. I want to sit. *(She sits on the ground. He does not.)*

MORGAN: I don't know that you want to sit on the floor, *per se.*

CORDELIA: I want to *stay* suspended.

MORGAN: You're wearing a very lovely —

CORDELIA: I want to be back in flight.

MORGAN: Why don't I go look for a restaurant?

CORDELIA: I was supposed to pick up groceries. I was supposed to make carrot soup. *I am so tired of carrot soup!*

MORGAN: So what do you want?

CORDELIA: I want caviar. I want oysters. I want ribs!

MORGAN: They're not here. That's why there's a car. We have to take a *Town Car* to get to . . . the things that we want.

CORDELIA: I thought I knew where I was going. On this trip. Through this life. And now I discover, I'm down a road; the past doesn't matter. I'm floating . . . I'm floating through my adult years! As a child I had purpose. As a child, I had coherence. I lived for a friend. I died for a grade. Now I live for what? Everything I know, I cling to. Family. I *cling*. Afraid to let go.

MORGAN: I would like the opportunity to work with you; on something. On anything.

CORDELIA: I don't see myself leaving.

MORGAN: I don't want this to slip away.

CORDELIA: I don't see myself leaving *here;* Any*thing;* any*one* —

(He sits with her.)

MORGAN: What *do* you see?

CORDELIA: A girl in flight.

MORGAN: She has to land.

CORDELIA: Not yet.

MORGAN: So where is she going? What does she want?

CORDELIA: She wants to stop flailing. She wants to stop struggling. She wants to curl up in a ball. She wants to love and be loved. She wants her mother. She wants her mother to see her happy with her daughter.

MORGAN: Of course she does.

CORDELIA: She wants to see her *husband* happy. Not worried. Or keeping secrets. He from her. She from him. Growing old. She wants them to be kids again in black-and-white photographs, carrying Italian army backpacks in T-shirts, looking for youth hostels in the countryside. Bringing the countryside to the city back with them. Never flying. Feet on the ground.

MORGAN: Good place for them to be.

CORDELIA: I want my family life sweet again.

MORGAN: Why can't it be? What's wrong with the photograph?

CORDELIA: We've betrayed each other.

MORGAN: How do you know?

CORDELIA: I know. This I know. I, him. He, me.

MORGAN: And is that why you're here, Cordelia?

CORDELIA: We've been flying separate flights; too long. . . . I loved that feeling today. At the cemetery. It was so full. And I knew no one!

MORGAN: Now you do. You've met someone.

CORDELIA: I have.

MORGAN: You can't go backwards. Pictures need to be replaced. We can't live in old black-and-white photos.

CORDELIA: Is that why you're replacing all the art in your boardroom?

MORGAN: Already have. It's gone. Garbage.

CORDELIA: I don't understand.

MORGAN: A room full of portraits. A life of richness and riches. And slowly, they bleed themselves dry. The portraits become old and empty, because there is a sickness imbedded; and the sickness eats away at the frame; at the body; at the soul; and then the memory. Until there is truly nothing left. Except the stench of loss. This I realize at lunch, alone in my boardroom, steak knife in my hand; I walk over to the paintings, and I hack them. I hack them to shreds. Into ribbons. This all of a week ago. Two years to the day after losing . . . After loss. And now I have empty frames of broken wood and scars in the paneling where a painting used to be. That was the first day I cried. Since Damon. Today's the second. *(She gets up.)* You probably hate me now.

CORDELIA: No.

MORGAN: Destroying things? Destroying art?

CORDELIA: Loss is devastating.

MORGAN: Yes.

CORDELIA: A signal, you said. That change is inevitable.

MORGAN: That we have no control.

CORDELIA: A plane could fall from the sky.

MORGAN: Any second.

CORDELIA: "Wind shears."

MORGAN: It has to change course, or it falls.

CORDELIA: But how does it know? Where to go?

MORGAN: It's called Radar.

CORDELIA: I don't have one.

MORGAN: No one does.

CORDELIA: So how does *anyone* know? When to change? Who with?

MORGAN: That's the drama . . . We don't.

(As Cordelia and Morgan kiss. For a very long time.)

CORDELIA: Point me.

MORGAN: Where?

CORDELIA: On a path.

MORGAN: What direction?

CORDELIA: Home.

MORGAN: And Home is? West Side? East Side? Midtown? Brooklyn?

CORDELIA: More choices.

MORGAN: Old. New. Same. Change. Home. Happiness?

CORDELIA: Home *is* happiness.

MORGAN: For some.

CORDELIA: It's peaceful *here*.

MORGAN: We can't *stay* here, Cordelia. We have to move.

(Cordelia breaks away.)

CORDELIA: . . . About your boardroom. Don't cover anything. Keep the scars. What you're looking for, it seems to me, is a room of multiple textures. Pain and light. Side by side. Colored sandstone. Rusted metal. Flecks of ochre. Old. New. A room of layers.

MORGAN: I like the idea. Of layers.

CORDELIA: A life made up of them.

MORGAN: . . . I'd say we're about to close down this terminal.

CORDELIA: Do you feel the breeze?

(Stepping forward.)

In my fantasy, I don't have to be in a drama. There are no stakes. The heart is open, and one is aware of all the layers of love in one's life, and it doesn't have to be confusing. It can be a blessing . . .

MORGAN: *(Offering the cell.)* Here. Let him know you're running late.

CORDELIA: I'm not running anywhere . . .

MORGAN: *(Putting the cell away.)* . . . Tell Luis to take you home. Wherever it is you're going. He'll get you there.

CORDELIA: Did you know, if you look up at this sky, then close your eyes, you can see the planets beckon in all directions?

(She puts her hands over Morgan's eyes. He gazes up. She removes her hands.)

Now open.

MORGAN: Pretty picture.

CORDELIA: You can keep it.

(Morgan looks at Cordelia, and she at him, and then he exits. Fade.)

END OF PLAY

HAPPENSTANCE

by Peter Sagal

HAPPENSTANCE

O'Hare International Airport, Chicago. United Terminal. C Concourse. Near Gate C-23. Martin sits on a bench, mid-thirties, wearing a rumpled suit, obviously nervous. He stands. He sits again. He picks up a paper, starts to read it. Puts it down. Pulls out a cell phone, puts it to his ear. Looks off into the distance, as if listening. Tries a few nods, as if following along with somebody.

MARTIN: Yes. We'll do that.

(Puts the phone back in his pocket. Tries the paper again. Does his best to look casual. Looks to his left; starts craning his head as if trying to pick someone out of a crowd. Sees that person. Stares. Tries not to. Picks up the paper again, at the last moment, and manages a look of utter distraction, just as Amy, thirties, dressed casually, walks by.

MARTIN: *(Surprised.)* Amy?

AMY: Martin!

(The look at each other.)

AMY: What a . . .

MARTIN: I mean, *once* was crazy enough . . .

AMY: Coincidence, exactly. Wow. You're . . .

MARTIN: Heading home. And you . . .

AMY: Yeah. A week in Albuquerque. And you were . . .

MARTIN: St. Paul. Was it a good time?

AMY: Fine. Yeah.

(Pause.)

Wow. I mean, I wonder if something is going on . . .

MARTIN: Like what?

AMY: I mean . . . I see you, first time in forever, in an airport, for god's sakes, and then, one week later . . .

MARTIN: It's O'Hare. Busiest airport in the world. Wait here long enough, you'd meet J.D. Salinger.

AMY: But still. Twice in a week? Not happenstance.

MARTIN: Happen . . . ?

AMY: I read it once. Once is happenstance. Twice is coincidence. Three times is enemy action.

MARTIN: Let's not do this again, then.

(Pause.)

AMY: St. Paul was good?

MARTIN: I don't know. Was it? Was I there? I always feel like I'm checking into different rooms at the same hotel.

AMY: I actually am. My company books with Marriot exclusively. You stay a certain minimum number of times, you get to become a Mormon.
(Pause.)

MARTIN: You're not a . . .

AMY: No. Marriot is owned by Mormons. And, um. They recruit heavily out of Brigham Young, so the senior staff is also . . . primarily . . . it was really, just a joke.

MARTIN: I had forgotten . . . how *smart* you are.

AMY: I'm not. I just have a lot of things to say.
(Pause.)

MARTIN: Well. Seeing as fate has cast us into each other's . . . company again, shall we tee up another drink? I've got our usual table reserved at the Fly-away Lounge.

AMY: It's a little early for me . . . I'm an hour behind.

MARTIN: Well. Sure. How about a cup of coffee, then?

AMY: Actually, I don't have that much of a layover, this time. Twenty minutes before my flight home.

MARTIN: Oh.

AMY: I told you that.

MARTIN: You did?

AMY: I was bitching about my layover, and then I said that I was glad I'd only have thirty minutes on the way back. And you said, there's no such thing as minutes at O'Hare. The minimum increment of time is three hours. It was a good line.

MARTIN: So . . . uh . . .

AMY: So I still got your card. Did I give you mine?

MARTIN: You might've. I don't . . .

AMY: Here.
(She gives him a card.)

MARTIN: Where's your flight? In this terminal?

AMY: Gate B-14.

MARTIN: Yeah, that's . . . that's the other terminal. You can see it through the window there.

AMY: Oh. How do I get from . . .

MARTIN: There's a tunnel, with a people mover. Stand on the left. It's really kind of cool, they did up these big neon musical tubes to distract you from the fact that you're lugging your bags half a mile, and it's kind of got this enameled plastic paneling from Logan's Run, it's like, the Airline Terminal of Tomorrow ride at Disneyland.

AMY: Sounds like fun. Well. It was great to see you again, again.

(Pause.)

MARTIN: My flight isn't for another hour, I'm just killing time, I can walk you over there. *(Pause.)* Always a treat to see the Neon People Mover.

AMY: I thought you were going home Wednesday.

MARTIN: I was, yes.

AMY: Something came up? Held you over?

MARTIN: You know how it is, you spend the whole day doing a meeting, the only thing you decide is to have another meeting. Things drag out.

AMY: For three whole days?

MARTIN: Stuff like this, you can't say no. You just have to . . . surrender.

AMY: Your wife must have been upset.

MARTIN: She was.

AMY: And your kids.

MARTIN: Did I tell you about them?

AMY: Yes.

MARTIN: I don't think they miss me too much anymore. I'm just the stand-by chauffeur. Do you have kids?

AMY: No, Martin. I told you that. *(Pause.)* I'm sorry you got held up. Get home safe. *(She turns and starts to walk away.)*

MARTIN: Amy! Um. *(Pause.)* It was so great to see you again. *Great.* It made me think, how so much is out of our control. If I had wanted to see you again . . . after so long . . . I couldn't have done it. Because of the *effort.* The trouble you have to go to . . . says too much. To like, call up the people I know who might know you, to track down your numbers. Then I'd call you up, I'd say, Hey, Amy, it's Martin, how are you, hey, I just was thinking of you, thought I'd call you up. You wouldn't believe me.

AMY: You're right. I wouldn't.

MARTIN: So. If something just *happens* . . . if you don't have to explain it to anyone . . . then maybe you should just take advantage of it.

AMY: Because nobody has to believe you.

MARTIN: Right.

(Pause.)

AMY: I don't believe you, Martin.

MARTIN: You don't believe . . . you don't believe . . .

AMY: Where's your laptop?

MARTIN: My. Oh, my . . .

AMY: Last week, you didn't let it get more than a foot from your right hand. Where is it?

(Pause. They both look around the seat where he's been.)

MARTIN: Oh, SHIT! It's been stolen!

(Pause. Neither of them does anything. Neither of them laughs.)

MARTIN: It's back at the hotel room.

AMY: The hotel room.

MARTIN: At the airport Hilton. I've been there for three days.

(Pause.)

AMY: A place in the city would have been nicer.

MARTIN: This was the only place in the whole world where I knew you'd be. Someday.

(Pause.)

AMY: I should go, Martin. I'm sorry for . . . for the wait.

MARTIN: No, no. I enjoyed it. Peace and quiet. Very good soundproofing. You know what's the amazing thing about the Airport Hilton? They've got all these, like, theme restaurants. With these pictures in front, of like these attractive couples stepping up to the bar, or at a table, as if they said to themselves, Hey, I'm in the mood for a romantic tête-à-tête, let's get out the ol' Mercedes and cruise on up to the fucking Airport Hilton; basically I'm desperate for you not to walk away.

(Pause.)

AMY: But I really should.

MARTIN: I thought you were glad to see me.

AMY: Glad is a strong word.

MARTIN: But not now.

AMY: I was happy to see you. To see you doing so well. That you had gotten married.

MARTIN: You thought I wouldn't.

AMY: I made no predictions.

MARTIN: Nobody would have me?

AMY: I was afraid you'd refuse, that you'd sit in your room for the rest of your life, just to make a point.

MARTIN: What would the point be?

AMY: What would it matter?

MARTIN: I didn't. I got up, and I moved on. I did. Every day, I do that.

AMY: Good for you. Speaking of which.

MARTIN: But I was never moving towards something. Only away. I felt like I've spent the past decade . . . receding.

AMY: Looking back. It's a mistake.

MARTIN: Sure. You look forward. You square your shoulders. And you still feel what happened on the back of your neck. Don't you . . . don't you think . . .

AMY: No.

MARTIN: You didn't know what I was going to say.

AMY: I don't agree, whatever it is. Because whatever it is, it's too late and too old and I have to catch a plane.

MARTIN: I should've . . .

AMY: You shouldn't have done anything different.

MARTIN: But I ruined things. I drove you away.

AMY: So what? You drove me away, and I was upset and then I got through it and I transferred to another program, and met a guy and then another guy, and then I got this job, and I have my life. And you have yours. Is that what you waited for? For three days in an airport hotel, so you could apologize for your entire life?

MARTIN: Yes.

AMY: Why?

MARTIN: Because it should have been something else. I fit in it wrong. I keep thinking . . . I had my life. And I let it go. And then it showed up again, at O'Hare airport. Where: I told you. Everybody shows up eventually.

AMY: What did you expect me to do?

MARTIN: You said you weren't married.

AMY: You said you were.

MARTIN: That's right. But why aren't you?

AMY: You think that I was waiting for you? That I was ruined because I couldn't have you? That every man I met, every word he said, every opinion he offered, I couldn't help compare it to yours and find it lacking? That on those few times that I swallowed enough bile to spend the night I couldn't help but stare at their pale bodies and think, "This is wrong, this is not what he looks like, this is incorrect." Is that what you thought?

MARTIN: That's how I feel.

AMY: Me too.

MARTIN: Amy . . . !

AMY: But not about you. The next guy. His name was Anthony. He was a writer. Traveled the world. I went with him. I told him I wanted to get married, wanted to have children. He said no, and left.

MARTIN: You never wanted to get married, and have kids.

AMY: Not with you.

(Pause.)

MARTIN: So maybe you do understand. All these years . . .

AMY: Every second of them. *(Pause.)* I'm going to miss my flight.

MARTIN: Amy . . .

AMY: Come on now . . .

MARTIN: There he is!

AMY: Who?

MARTIN: Your writer. There.

(She turns; then realizes he can't know. Turns back.)

MARTIN: He's flying back from Afghanistan. Rucksack on his shoulder. He sees you, and his eyebrows go up and he smiles so wide . . .

(She turns and looks, as if the person were there.)

MARTIN: That you know . . . that if he's thought about you at all in the endless years since you saw him . . . it didn't hurt him. And you try to be non-chalant, and you *know* that your job here is to make him understand that it didn't matter, that without him your life was fine, that you survived him, that you're better off. And you realize, as you natter on about your wife and your kids and your job, that he couldn't give a fuck. Because he hasn't thought about you twice.

And he goes, and it all comes back, the CERTAINTY that you blew it. Your whole life. And guess what: you blew it again. So you say: give me one more chance. I'll do anything. I won't let him walk away again.

AMY: But I do.

MARTIN: Which I did. But I figured: one more chance. Then, finally, I'll be ready.

(Pause. She turns to go.)

MARTIN: Hey, Amy? If you did see him . . . the last time. What would you want him to say?

(Pause. Amy considers.)

AMY: Hey. I've been thinking about you.

MARTIN: A lot?

AMY: No. Just . . . have you heard that the Universe is spreading apart? They used to think that someday it would slow down, stop, start falling together again. Which was always comforting to me. Even if I didn't get to see it. All of it . . . everywhere . . . would fall back in with everything else, and have another start. But not anymore. Now everything's just going to run away from each other, forever. And every second, things get further away, and we'll never go there. Every moment more and more places become impossible.

MARTIN: Sad thought.

AMY: Yeah. But then I think . . . wasn't it lucky? That we were at least able to look up in time, and see it all? Even if we'll never be able to go?

MARTIN: I don't know.

AMY: I do. I'm glad to know you're out there. Going away.

(Long pause.)

MARTIN: So. See you around, huh?

AMY: It was good to see you, Martin. You look great. Just like I remember.

(She leaves. Martin takes out her business card. And drops it on the floor. Lights fade.)

END OF PLAY

LAYOVER

by Joe Sutton

CHARACTERS

ALEX, a very young man.

LIZA, his girlfriend.

SHELDON, a man in his forties.

ELLEN, Sheldon's wife as she was twenty years ago.

CHRISTINE, a woman in her thirties.

PLACE

An airport lounge.

TIME

The present.

LAYOVER

An airport lounge. Lisa and Alex, two lovers in their twenties, are wrapped in each other's arms barely able to keep their hands off each other. They stare deep in each other's eyes, as Sheldon, a man in his forties, sits down the row from them trying to read a book. They communicate in breathy whispers.

LIZA: It's been ten minutes.

ALEX: Since?

LIZA: You said it.

ALEX: Said . . . ?

LIZA: I love you.
(He smiles.)

ALEX: *(Beat.)* I love you.

LIZA: How much?

ALEX: Enough to have your children.

LIZA: That's . . . *(Now it's she who smiles.)* . . . you're going to have the children?

ALEX: *(Playful.)* Yes. That's how much I love you.
(Then.)

LIZA: And before that?

ALEX: Before . . .?

LIZA: Before you have the children. What else?

ALEX: *(Confused.)* What . . .?

LIZA: How else will you show it? Your love.

ALEX: Well, there will be displays.

LIZA: Displays?

ALEX: Of love, yes. Physical displays.

LIZA: Of what sort?

ALEX: Kissing. For starters. There will be lots . . . of kissing.

LIZA: *(Becoming aroused.)* Where?

ALEX: In airports. At terminal gates. In chairs.
(The two start to kiss. It's a tentative kiss that soon becomes very sexy — then suddenly stops.)

LIZA: *(Then, after a moment.)* What else?

ALEX: What other displays?

LIZA: Yes.

ALEX: In public?

LIZA: Yes.

ALEX: Well —

(Alex starts to reach for her when Sheldon, who has been listening throughout, suddenly turns on them and explodes.)

SHELDON: Excuse me!

(And the two lovers look at him — causing Sheldon to pull back.)

SHELDON: Pardon me, I'm sorry, I . . .

(He now withdraws even further, embarrassed.)

SHELDON: Do you have the time?

(The young man stares at him in disbelief — before shaking his head.)

ALEX: No.

SHELDON: *(Still embarrassed.)* I'm sorry.

(Alex then returns his attention to Liza — who laughs.)

ALEX: *(Then, after a beat.)* Mostly it will be kissing. But there will be times when we're very careful, and discreet —

(Suddenly, the older man turns on the audience, his memories coming out in a torrent. Meanwhile, behind him, the lovers are frozen in place.)

SHELDON: I remember once when I was on a bus. I was with a woman I thought I would marry and we started kissing. Right there in the middle of the bus, standing up. It was the most delicious, passionate . . . watery moment of my life. And I got very aroused. So aroused that I realized . . . halfway through the kiss I was . . . that there was likely to be evidence. A spot. And I was embarrassed. But I couldn't stop kissing.

(Once again, the lovers come to life.)

LIZA: *(Husky.)* Tell me the things.

ALEX: What things?

LIZA: About me. *(Beat.)* That you love.

ALEX: Your touch. *(Taking his time.)* I love your touch. Your laugh. That you let me say things. When we're talking . . . when we're together you let me say things, tell you things that I'm thinking about, you . . . *(Realizing what he's been trying to say.)* . . . I feel smart.

LIZA: You *are* smart.

(He smiles.)

ALEX: Your eyes.

LIZA: *(After a moment.)* Your breath. It's warm and sweet and sometimes just a little bit bad. Like you.

ALEX: Am I bad?

LIZA: A little.

ALEX: How?

LIZA: When you make me do things I don't want to do. That I've never done before. Till I find out I like them.

ALEX: Like?

LIZA: This. Making love in public.

ALEX: Are we making love?

LIZA: We're starting to.

ALEX: Will we finish?

LIZA: If you like.

(Beat.)

ALEX: Let's get down on the floor.

SHELDON: *(Again exploding.)* Excuse me, I'm sorry. I'm . . .

(The man is now bursting with indignation.)

SHELDON: This is a public place. *(Sputtering.)* Do you . . .? *(Wanting their concurrence.)* Right??? *(He waits, but they don't reply.)* Please.

(Sheldon then turns to the audience, the lovers once again freezing in place.)

SHELDON: They didn't look at me. They were staring at, but . . . they didn't look. Or they didn't see I guess is more like it. I wasn't there for them. I was just . . . a voice. A voice they didn't want or need to hear.

(Just then, Ellen, a young woman in her twenties, enters wearing a pantsuit from the seventies. She is his wife as she appeared twenty years ago, and she is very annoyed.)

ELLEN: Sheldon?

SHELDON: *(Turning, startled.)* Yes.

ELLEN: What are you doing?

SHELDON: What?

ELLEN: *(Sharply.)* What are you doing?

SHELDON: *(Defensive.)* Looking out.

ELLEN: At what?

SHELDON: The hills. The clouds.

ELLEN: *(Momentarily concerned.)* Are you all right?

SHELDON: Yes.

ELLEN: *(Once again angry.)* Am I boring you?

SHELDON: No.

ELLEN: I thought you wanted to talk about this.

SHELDON: I do! *(Confused.)* What?

ELLEN: Where we're seating everyone.

SHELDON: Oh. Right.

ELLEN: Now, I thought —

SHELDON: Ellen?

ELLEN: Yes.

SHELDON: Will you kiss me?

ELLEN: What!

SHELDON: Give me a kiss.

ELLEN: Sheldon we're on a plane.

SHELDON: I know.

ELLEN: There are people!

SHELDON: I know.

(Ellen looks at him crossly, then kisses him, impulsively, on the cheek.)

SHELDON: No. Not like that.

ELLEN: Sheldon, I'm not . . . we're on a plane!

(She is now getting really annoyed.)

SHELDON: I know.

ELLEN: Well, I'm not —

SHELDON: We were on a bus not long ago.

ELLEN: And that . . . I lost my head.

SHELDON: Lose it again.

(Ellen stares at him for a moment, then suddenly lunges at him, the two starting to kiss, when suddenly the boy yells out in pain.)

ALEX: Ow!

(He then spins on Sheldon.)

ALEX: Sir. Sir!

(And Sheldon turns to him.)

SHELDON: What?

ALEX: You're stepping on my hand.

(By now Ellen has disappeared — and Sheldon moves his foot.)

SHELDON: I'm sorry.

(Alex then withdraws his hand, staring at Sheldon.)

ALEX: Listen, do you think you could move?

SHELDON: What?

ALEX: *(Bluntly.)* Could you find somewhere else to sit? This is kind of a private place here, and . . . could you find somewhere else?

(Sheldon is crushed.)

SHELDON: Sure.

ALEX: *(Sharp.)* Thanks.

(Alex then watches as Sheldon picks up his bag and crosses to a seat just a few rows away.)

ALEX: Actually —

LIZA: *(Interrupting.)* Alex.

ALEX: *(Turning.)* What?

LIZA: Forget it.

(She shrugs. He then turns back to her after staring hard at Sheldon.)

ALEX: I don't believe this.

LIZA: Give me your coat.

(Sheldon then turns to the audience.)

SHELDON: And the boy then gave her his coat and the two . . . then proceeded to do it. Or actually I wasn't sure what they were doing exactly. It just *seemed* like they were doing it. *(Beat.)* And I watched them.

(Suddenly Ellen is once again at his side, the sound of a train's clickety-clack running beneath their conversation.)

ELLEN: *(Determined.)* No.

SHELDON: What?

ELLEN: No. I . . . *(She shakes her head vehemently.)* . . . no.

SHELDON: Ellen, no one can see us.

ELLEN: I don't care.

SHELDON: We're all alone!

ELLEN: It doesn't matter.

SHELDON: That's why —

ELLEN: Did you bring cards?

SHELDON: *(Annoyed.)* What?

ELLEN: Did you bring cards?

SHELDON: Ellen, why did we do this? Didn't we do this, in part, for this?

ELLEN: Let's wait till we get home.

(Suddenly Sheldon turns to the lovers, now lying spent on the floor.)

SHELDON: Excuse me!

(And Alex looks up, or over his head actually at Sheldon who is sitting behind him.)

ALEX: Yeah?

(As once again Ellen has disappeared.)

SHELDON: *(Suddenly self-conscious.)* I watched you.

ALEX: *(Confused.)* What?

SHELDON: Just now. I . . . watched you.

ALEX: And?

SHELDON: *(Beat.)* Your wife, may I talk to her?

(Alex shrugs.)

LIZA: Yeah?

SHELDON: Are you embarrassed?

LIZA: By what?

SHELDON: *(Himself embarrassed.)* Making love. In public.

LIZA: No. I'm not embarrassed.

(And now Ellen reappears.)

ELLEN: And I *was.* So what?

SHELDON: So it's perfectly natural. *(To Liza.)* Right?

LIZA: Yeah.

SHELDON: The man is with his wife. He feels passion for her, he wants to express himself. What's wrong with that?

ELLEN: Nothing. It just wasn't me.

(And this stumps him. Sheldon then turns back to Alex, who also shrugs his shoulder.)

ALEX: That's not what you had.

SHELDON: *(Exasperated.)* I *know* that's not what we had. *(Then.)* That's not what we *have.*

LIZA: What *do* you have?

SHELDON: *(To Ellen.)* What *do* we have?

ELLEN: A marriage, Sheldon. A normal marriage.

SHELDON: *(To the kids.)* A normal marriage.

ALEX: And you want more?

SHELDON: *(Emphatic.)* Yes! *(Then, suddenly wondering.)* Or . . . I don't know.

ELLEN: *(Exasperated herself.)* Sheldon, I'm forty-six. You're forty-six. What do you want?

SHELDON: Passion.

(This last he says to the audience, turning out.)

SHELDON: But I say that I sound like a moron. *(Then, back to Ellen.)* I don't know.

ELLEN: *(Angry.)* Well, think about it. Okay? With all this fantasizing you're doing . . . *(Sharp.)* . . . think about it!

(Suddenly the stage darkens and Christine, a woman in her thirties, comes out. Sheldon immediately backs away.)

CHRISTINE: *(Drunken, seductive.)* That was "nice."

SHELDON: Yeah, well —

CHRISTINE: Let's do it again.

(Sheldon laughs nervously, shaking his head.)

SHELDON: I —

CHRISTINE: Don't you want to?

SHELDON: I do, yes, but —

CHRISTINE: You're scared.

SHELDON: Yes.

CHRISTINE: Don't be.

(She advances on him.)

SHELDON: Listen, I made a mistake.

CHRISTINE: I didn't.

SHELDON: We could get in trouble!

CHRISTINE: Who with?

SHELDON: The office . . . *(His mind racing.)* . . . everyone!

CHRISTINE: Only if we tell. *(Beat, husky, and now very close.)* Are we gonna tell?

SHELDON: *(Beat, surrendering.)* No.

(She comes closer.)

CHRISTINE: Come here.

(With that, she starts kissing him, her kiss as sloppy and passionate as his is hesitant. Then suddenly she breaks away.)

CHRISTINE: *(Aroused.)* Let's go upstairs.

SHELDON: *(Alarmed.)* What?

CHRISTINE: To your room.

SHELDON: No! I mean . . . I can't.

CHRISTINE: Why not?

SHELDON: *(Stammering.)* I . . . have to . . . there's —

CHRISTINE: *(Frustrated.)* What!

SHELDON: I have to call home. *(Repeating himself, trying to convince.)* I promised I would call home.

(Suddenly the kids reappear, both of them staring at Sheldon in disbelief.)

ALEX: *(Immediate.)* You did?

SHELDON: Yes.

ALEX: *(Incredulous.)* You called home??

SHELDON: Yes.

LIZA: Right there?

SHELDON: Yes.

ALEX: *(Shaking head.)* Jesus, Sheldon.

SHELDON: I . . . didn't know what else to do.

LIZA: *(Outraged.)* You coulda stayed. Right? You could have stayed with her.

SHELDON: I could have, yes.

(Quickly, the lights cross-fade to Ellen.)

ELLEN: *(Sharp.)* But you didn't.

SHELDON: No.

(She nods her head.)

ELLEN: I see. *(Then, after a moment.)* She called here, you know.

SHELDON: Who?

ELLEN: The girl. *(Beat.)* Christine.

SHELDON: *(Surprised.)* She called here?

ELLEN: Yes.

SHELDON: And said what?

ELLEN: That she was arriving. That she was in the city and you could call her if you wanted. *(Then.)* She said she was a colleague.

(Beat.)

SHELDON: You didn't tell me.

ELLEN: No. *(Icy.)* I didn't.

(Sheldon stares at her.)

SHELDON: *(Then.)* I'm sorry.

(And the kids once again appear.)

ALEX: And that was it? That was . . .

SHELDON: *(Nodding, nonplussed.)* That was it.

LIZA: You didn't . . . you never saw her again?

SHELDON: I saw her twice actually. She came to the office twice.

ALEX: But . . . nothing happened?

SHELDON: Nothing happened.

(Beat.)

LIZA: Will she come again?

SHELDON: Christine?

LIZA: Yes.

SHELDON: *(Beat.)* Yeah.

(Liza shrugs her shoulders as if to say, "Well?" Sheldon laughs nervously.)

SHELDON: I . . .

ALEX: Why not, Sheldon? If that's what you want, why not?

SHELDON: *(Loudly, protesting.)* Because it wasn't passion, it was alcohol. It was . . . it's not the same.

(Liza shrugs.)

LIZA: It's a start.

(Then, after a moment.)

LIZA: Anyway, that was our plane.

SHELDON: *(Confused.)* What?

LIZA: You're Chicago, right?

SHELDON: Yeah.

LIZA: That was our plane.

(Alex smiles, grabbing for his bag. He stands.)

ALEX: Are you okay?

SHELDON: *(Annoyed.)* What!

ALEX: You seem flushed. Are you —

SHELDON: *(Snapping.)* I'm fine! *(Then.)* Thanks.

   (Beat.)

ALEX: Sheldon, listen, don't . . . *(Taking another tack.)* . . . if you . . . *(Then, giving up.)* . . . never mind. *(He then raises his hand.)* See you.

   (And Liza, who also has her bag, waves as well.)

LIZA: See you.

   (And with that, the two leave — and Sheldon, for the first time, is alone. Taking a moment to recover, he then reaches for his bags only to suddenly reach for his coat instead. Removing a cellular phone from his pocket, he quickly punches in a number, gathering his bags together as he does.)

SHELDON: *(Then, into phone.)* Christine Hastert, please.

   (He then waits, turning in a circle, nervously patting his coat pockets until she answers. Finally . . .)

SHELDON: *(Into phone.)* Chrissy, hi, this is . . .

   (But as soon as he starts, he stops, unsure of how, or more important, whether, to proceed.)

SHELDON: *(Nervous.)* . . . um . . . *(By now having significant second thoughts.)* . . . this . . .

   (And suddenly, he hangs up, disconnecting the phone with his thumb and then lowering the phone. A long moment then passes before Sheldon finally lets out a breath, coming out when it does in a half-chuckle, half-snort of relief. Then . . .)

SHELDON: This is a man . . . *(He considers his statement.)* . . . this is a man . . . with a lot of time on his hands.

   (And with that, the lights slowly fade to black.)

END OF PLAY

CECILIA

by Jay Tarses

CECILIA

An airport waiting area. Two people are seated one or two seats apart. The woman of them is reading a book. No one else is in the area. Boarding announcements can be heard from time to time, but the language is garbled or foreign.

HIM: What do you think of my laptop?

SHE: Shut up.

HIM: I'm a playwright. I'm writing a play here at the airport.

SHE: Good. I'm reading a book.

HIM: What do you think of my laptop?

SHE: Please don't talk to me, okay?

HIM: Excuse me? I'm not talking to you.

SHE: Yes, you were.

HIM: I'm trying out some lines for my play. I'm a playwright. I wasn't talking to you. I don't NEED to talk to you. So leave me alone or I'll call security. I mean it.

SHE: You asked me what I thought of your laptop.

HIM: That was a line from my play. The Laptop Play.

SHE: You don't even HAVE a laptop.

HIM: Exactly. So please stop stalking me.

SHE: Stalking you? YOU were stalking ME. You were trying to get me to stare into your lap which you pretended was covered by a laptop and when I would gullibly look down, you would expose yourself.

HIM: Don't flatter yourself.

SHE: Don't flatter myself?

HIM: As if I'd expose myself to you. As if being a playwright's not enough. As if, in addition, I'd have to physically expose myself.

SHE: Do you mind if I read my book in peace and quiet. Until they call my plane. God . . . I can't wait to get out of this sick town.

HIM: What book are you reading?

SHE: None of your business.

HIM: What?

SHE: Don't ask me what book I'm reading.

HIM: I didn't.

SHE: You most certainly did.

HIM: Would you just leave me alone? Please! I beg you!

SHE: If you must know, it's about the Lewis and Clark Expedition.

HIM: What? What??

SHE: The book I'm reading is about the Lewis and Clark Expedition.

HIM: Hey! I don't care! I'm trying to write a play!

SHE: You asked me what book I was reading.

HIM: Should I just move? Is that what you want? Will that, at long last, get you to stop? Once and for all?

SHE: If you're writing a play, where's your paper, where's your pen, where's your typewriter, where's your laptop?

HIM: Ever heard of a tape recorder, you idiot! You're beneath contempt!

SHE: What's your name? If you're a playwright.

HIM: If I'm a playwright, what's my name. Does that follow? If you're a whore, what's YOUR name?

SHE: Have you written a play I would have heard of?

HIM: No . . . you're too much of an idiot to have heard of anything except the Lewis and Clark Expedition.

SHE: Well . . . I see. Okay. Fine. Hmm. Hasn't this little conversation gone and shifted on us subtly?

HIM: Yeah . . . from your being an idiot to your being a whore.

(There is an unintelligible boarding announcement.)

SHE: You've whetted my curiosity with your unorthodox "playwright" approach, or whatever you call it. And now, I'd like you to be part of my life. If only for a few minutes.

HIM: Why don't you go piss up a rope or something?

SHE: Do you know anything about Lewis and Clark?

HIM: I know about Lewis.

SHE: He committed suicide.

HIM: I didn't know that.

SHE: He was an alcoholic.

HIM: I didn't know that.

SHE: So there. There's much we could learn from one another.

HIM: Um. . . why do you think this is a sick town?

SHE: Because of all the hospitals.

HIM: You can't keep running away, Cecilia.

SHE: Cecilia?

HIM: What? Oh, sorry. Cecilia's the name of my heroine. She's trying to leave some sick town but she runs into a guy at the airport with a laptop. She doesn't actually run into him with a laptop. He HAS a laptop, but no one runs into it. Sound familiar?

SHE: All too.

HIM: You're my muse, you know. You're the reason for all of this.

(There is another garbled announcement.)

SHE: That's my plane.

HIM: Creevin? You're going to Creevin?

SHE: Oh . . . I thought they said Flayner.

HIM: No, Creevin. Where's Flayner?

SHE: North of Stalphin Junction. It's green and unspoiled.

HIM: I'll bet you're anxious to get home.

SHE: I am. People know me there. It's a town without hospitals. I've been away too long. And I should return this Lewis and Clark book to the Flayner public library.

HIM: This is crazy, isn't it? That this should happen to us here and now?

SHE: I know. It's like a wild, wonderful roller coaster ride. We might just as well be in a train station or a bus station or a boat station, but here we are in an airport station.

(Another announcement.)

SHE: *(Continuing.)* That was me. Flayner.

HIM: Flayner.

SHE: So.

HIM: Do you have any money?

SHE: Yes, I do.

HIM: Give it all to me.

SHE: What?

HIM: You heard me.

SHE: This is a line from your play?

HIM: I'm deadly serious. I have a gun. I'll think nothing of shooting you in the abdomen if I have to. Give me your money.

SHE: This whole bizarre afternoon's been bizarre. You're the most colorful person I've ever met. I wish . . . I wish we had more time.

HIM: What? Oh . . . yes. Right. More time.

SHE: Who knows where this could have taken us?

HIM: But we only had ten minutes.

SHE: Good-bye.

HIM: Are you sure you won't give me your money?

SHE: *(Shakes her head, sadly.)* Good-bye.

HIM: Good-bye, Cecilia.

(She exits. Blackout.)

END OF PLAY

Peanuts

by Tug Yourgrau

CHARACTERS

    GATE AGENT, woman, sixties.

    FRANCES, woman, seventies.

    HERB, seventies.

    MIRIAM, seventies.

    PHIL, forty-five.

PLACE

    The departure gate at a small airport. The check-in counter is up center. The door to the plane is up left. The seats are on the right facing the audience.

TIME

    3:30 P.M. The present.

NOTE

    Within dialogue:

    " . . ." indicates an ellipsis. The person stops speaking voluntarily.

    " — " indicates an interruption.

PEANUTS

Lights come up on Herb and Frances sitting in chairs. The Gate Agent is working behind the counter.

FRANCES: How many times do I have to keep telling you? *(Pause.)* You never listen.

(Pause.)

HERB: I didn't see him coming.

FRANCES: That's just what I mean.

(Pause.)

HERB: Well, there's no sense arguing about it now.

FRANCES: Sometimes you make me so angry! You are the most exasperating person I've ever . . . you never listen!

HERB: Frances, you gonna drive me nuts with this, can you please leave this alone?

FRANCES: No, I can't!

HERB: But it's over! There's nothing I can do anymore. For the lov'a Mike, will you please just let it go? *(Pause.)* It's over. It's done.

FRANCES: Yes, well, but there should have been more time, there could have been.

HERB: What do you want from me? How many times do I have to keep saying I'm sorry? I'm sorry, I made a mistake.

(Pause.)

FRANCES: It was so messy.

HERB: You think it's better any other way? It never is.

FRANCES: Well, I would have liked a chance to say a real good-bye to Judy and the kids.

HERB: Of course, so would I.

(Pause.)

FRANCES: Now we're going to miss the school play and the basketball games and her concert and their grad —

HERB: Are you trying to kill me, is that what you're trying to do?

(Pause.)

FRANCES: I'm just saying you I've told you a million times to watch out for —

HERB: Enough! *(Pause.)* Judy will be fine. Paul makes a good living, he's a good father.

FRANCES: Well, that's nice to hear for a change.

(Pause.)

HERB: I've never had a problem with Paul.

FRANCES: Oh, no, excuse me, but yes you have.

HERB: Well, that was at the beginning. When he was still up on his high horse.

FRANCES: Oh, come on, just last week I heard you tell him —

HERB: I just don't like it when he criticizes her.

FRANCES: You never liked him from the start.

HERB: Ach, nonsense.

FRANCES: No one was good enough for your little girl.

HERB: That's over, that's history.

FRANCES: Well, I don't know about that.

HERB: No, I've been thinking, they make a good match.

FRANCES: Well, I wish you'd let her know that before —

HERB: I did.

FRANCES: You did? When?

HERB: Last week.

FRANCES: When did you see her last week?

HERB: I didn't see her. We spoke on the phone.

FRANCES: Did you really?

HERB: Yes. So I'm not such a grump after all, am I?

FRANCES: Honey. *(Pause.)* I love you.

HERB: I love you too.

(He squeezes her hand. Miriam enters and goes to the counter.)

MIRIAM: Hello, is this the right gate for, is this the flight to — ?

GATE AGENT: May I just see your ticket, please? And a photo ID?

MIRIAM: A photo ID?

GATE AGENT: Yes, ma'am.

MIRIAM: For this flight?

GATE AGENT: FAA regulations.

MIRIAM: You're kidding.

GATE AGENT: A picture ID or I'm afraid I can't let you board.

MIRIAM: You can't let me on board?

(Pause. The Gate Agent looks at her.)

All right. All right.

(She finds the ID and hands it to the Agent.)

I look a little different from when this —

GATE AGENT: No problem. That's fine. *(She hands back the ID.)* How many bags?

MIRIAM: Just this.

GATE AGENT: Did anyone ask you to bring anything onto this flight for them?

MIRIAM: You're kidding me.

GATE AGENT: Did anyone ask you to — ?

MIRIAM: How could anyone ask me to bring something?

GATE AGENT: Just answer the question, please.

    (Pause.)

MIRIAM: No, they didn't.

GATE AGENT: And has your bag been in your sight at all times since you packed it?

MIRIAM: Are you really going to keep this up? *(Pause.)* No, I mean, yes, my bag has been in my sight the whole —

GATE AGENT: Thank you. Here's your boarding pass. We'll be boarding shortly.

    (Miriam takes a seat. Herb leans over to her.)

HERB: She did the same thing to us.

MIRIAM: It's ridiculous.

HERB: What are you going to do? Who you gonna complain to?

MIRIAM: Well, when we get there, I certainly plan to say something.

    (Pause.)

FRANCES: You're traveling . . . by yourself?

MIRIAM: Yes.

FRANCES: Oh, I see.

    (Pause.)

MIRIAM: I've been sick for the last couple of months.

FRANCES: Uh, huh.

MIRIAM: Then I got pneumonia, and . . . you know.

FRANCES: Of course. We were very sick, both of us, earlier this year.

MIRIAM: And that's what . . . ?

HERB: No, no. Traffic.

MIRIAM: Oh, yes.

HERB: What're you gonna do? The car is the most dangerous mode of transportation there is.

FRANCES: Especially the way you drive.

HERB: Frances!

FRANCES: Well, it's true.

    (Pause.)

MIRIAM: I'm going to see my Billy. I haven't seen him in four years.

FRANCES: Oh, that's wonderful. You must be so excited.

MIRIAM: I feel like I've waited forever. It's been hard, very hard.

HERB: No one ever said it would be easy. No one ever said it would. You know, this reminds me, back in the thirties, in Dorchester. You know Dorchester?

MIRIAM: Oh, yes.

HERB: Well, back then, the Jews and Irish, we ran everything. Together. Bishop Flanagan — you remember Bishop Flanagan?

MIRIAM: Oh, yes.

HERB: What a man, marvelous man. His right hand man was Izzy Levine. Oh yes, those were the days. My father and uncle started up the credit union, the WASP bankers, BankBoston, Shawmut, they wouldn't lend a dime to the Jews. Or the Irish.

FRANCES: Herbie, Herbie.

HERB: What?

MIRIAM: No, I remember those days.

HERB: Oh, I tell you, don't get me started on the WASPs. Oh, those bastards. You're never good enough for them. They're always sniffing shit when they see the Jews or the Irish, even the Italians. And Harvard! Harvard's the worst. And the Harvard Jews, they're worse than the WASPs.

FRANCES: Stop it, Herbert.

HERB: What? Anyway, where was I? Oh, yes, Shaugnessy, Father Shaugnessy. Wonderful man. Built small, but oh was he tough. Came from Brick-bottom over there in Cambridge. Those Brickbottom Irish are tough. He boxed in high school, won thirteen fights. Played football at Holy Cross. Guard or tackle, I can't remember, imagine, at his size. Anyway, he became a priest at Most Blessed Sacrament, the people loved him. Bishop Flana-gan was taking notice and then, one night, I'll remember it to this day, he slipped in the bathtub and broke his neck. Broke his neck! Just twenty-eight years old. So for the next thirty-four years, he has to wear a neck brace and some kind of rod thing for his back every day. Imagine, this athlete. The pain was agonizing.

FRANCES: Herbie, Herbie!

HERB: What?

FRANCES: I'm sure the lady doesn't want to listen to your stories about —

MIRIAM: Oh, no, that's all right, I don't mind.

HERB: What? We were just talking about how it's never easy. I'm saying Father Shaugnessy —

FRANCES: Settle down. Give the lady some room.

HERB: What?

MIRIAM: It's Okay.

(Phil enters with a cell phone to his ear.)

PHIL: Hello? Hello? *(He fusses with the phone as he goes to the counter and fumbles for his ticket and ID.)* Hello? *(The phone still doesn't work.)* Jesus!

HERB: Young man in a hurry.

FRANCES: Ssh!

PHIL: Exit row aisle, please.

GATE AGENT: Photo ID please.

PHIL: Do you have my frequent flier number?

(The Gate Agent checks in the computer.)

HERB: Oh, my God!

FRANCES: Herbie! Quiet.

GATE AGENT: Yessir, it's already in the system.

PHIL: And what are we flying today?

GATE AGENT: A Beechcraft 27.

PHIL: Beechcraft?

GATE AGENT: Yessir.

(Phil stares out the window.)

PHIL: That's the plane?

GATE AGENT: Yessir.

PHIL: A propeller?

GATE AGENT: Yessir.

PHIL: Oh, man, my travel agent must have messed up. Is there a later flight out?

(Herb laughs.)

FRANCES: Sssh!

GATE AGENT: No, sir, this is the only flight today.

PHIL: Jeez, flying in a can of tuna. How much longer does this take than the regular flight?

GATE AGENT: Oh, it's the same.

PHIL: The same? A jet and a propeller?

GATE AGENT: Yessir.

PHIL: How can that be?

GATE AGENT: Sir, the flight takes the same amount of time.

PHIL: All right, if you say so.

(He goes and sits down near Miriam.)

PHIL: Did you know this was a prop, the plane is a propeller, it's not a jet?

MIRIAM: Oh, it doesn't matter.

PHIL: Well, have you flown in one recently?

MIRIAM: Oh, young man, that's all there used to be.

PHIL: Yes, well, no, I mean, I just wish I'd known, that's all. *(He pulls out a laptop and plugs it in. He tries his cell phone again.)* I can't believe it, this is a brand new . . .

MIRIAM: Oh, well, I could never figure out how to use those things.

HERB: Who you gonna call anyway?

FRANCES: Herbert!

PHIL: Excuse me?

FRANCES: Herbie, stop it.

HERB: What? I'm just asking the man who he thinks he's calling.

FRANCES: Just ignore my husband, he hasn't been well.

PHIL: Oh, that's all right.

HERB: So tell me, who're you calling?

PHIL: Well, since you asked. I'm calling this theater in Greenwich Village I work with. It's a bunch of playwrights, *working* playwrights. Every year we put on a festival of one-acts and tonight's the night we're reading them through to each other. I'm calling to tell them I'll be late.

HERB: And how!

(Herbie barely stifles a laugh.)

MIRIAM: Oh, so you're in the theater?

PHIL: Yes, among other things.

HERB: You talk about theater, I remember the old days, that was theatre, not this mischpisch they have nowadays.

FRANCES: Oh, shush.

HERB: I remember seeing, it must have been 1949, Arthur Miller's *Death of a Salesman* at the Schubert Theatre on Tremont Street. You talk about theater. That was a performance I'll never forget it. Karl Malden played Willy Loman.

FRANCES: No, not Karl Malden!

HERB: Yes, Karl Malden.

FRANCES: Karl Malden never played Willy Loman.

HERB: In Boston he did. I saw him.

FRANCES: It was Lee Jay Cobb.

HERB: No, it wasn't.

FRANCES: Yes, it was.

MIRIAM: You said you did something else. What else did you do?

PHIL: Oh, I'm a, it's a, I have a small company, we make videos and films. Documentaries mostly.

FRANCES: Oh, nature films?

PHIL: No, no, forensic science actually. You know, how the police use science to solve murders, that sort of thing.

MIRIAM: Oh, is that on the cable?

PHIL: Yes. Yes, it is.

MIRIAM: Oh, I don't get cable.

PHIL: Well, you're probably better off reading a book anyway.

MIRIAM: That's my favorite channel. I watch all the nature shows.

PHIL: Yes, well . . . anyway, excuse me, I have to finish this thing for tonight.

(Herbie laughs and claps his hands.)

FRANCES: Herbie!

PHIL: You know, I wish you'd let me know just what's so funny.

FRANCES: Oh, don't mind my husband, he doesn't mean badly.

PHIL: Well . . .

(He starts typing. Pause.)

MIRIAM: Young man, do you know where this flight is going?

PHIL: Yes, ma'am, I know where this flight's going.

(Herbie stifles a laugh.)

MIRIAM: You're sure?

PHIL: Yes, I'm sure. Look, if you'll excuse me, I've got to get some work done.

(He gets up, gathers his things, and shifts to faraway seat. Pause.)

HERB: Someone should tell him.

FRANCES: Just leave it alone.

HERB: No, someone ought to tell him. *(He walks over to Phil.)* Young man, do you know where you're going?

PHIL: Good lord!

HERB: Now just hold your horses for a second, we're trying to tell you something. How did you get here?

PHIL: How did I get here?

HERB: Yes, how did you get to the airport?

PHIL: I drove.

HERB: And what happened?

PHIL: What happened? I drove down Route 1, I got off at the airport exit, and I was going around the circle when this huge truck suddenly . . . *(Pause.)* Oh, my God.

(The Gate Agent moves to the door of the departure gate and speaks into a microphone.)

GATE AGENT: Thank you for your patience, ladies and gentlemen. Our flight is now ready for boarding. Please have your boarding passes out and available.

FRANCES: Herbie!

HERB: What now?

PHIL: You shouldn't tell him just like that. It's a shock.

HERB: What? He should know.

PHIL: My God.

MIRIAM: It's going to be Okay.

> *(Pause.)*

PHIL: And you're all, all of you are . . . ?

FRANCES: Yes.

HERB: That's right.

MIRIAM: I'm going to see my Billy. We were married for forty-six years.

HERB: With us it was also an accident. Cars, I tell you. An airplane, now that's the safest way you can travel.

PHIL: This is it?

HERB: Why not?

PHIL: But I never expected it to be like this.

MIRIAM: A train would only take longer.

PHIL: But I can't, it can't be me. There must be some mistake. This plane's going to New York.

HERB: In a way it still is.

MIRIAM: When we land, they'll tell us what the connecting flight is to, you know, the other places.

FRANCES: Didn't they tell you all this when you . . . ?

PHIL: But I'm not ready to, I'm too young. I mean, my wife, my kids, my God!

MIRIAM: Oh, what a shame.

FRANCES: Yes, it comes as a shock.

HERB: Nothing you can do about it now, pal.

FRANCES: Herbert!

HERB: Well, there isn't.

FRANCES: That's not what he wants to hear now. How many children do you have?

PHIL: What?

FRANCES: I said, how many — ?

PHIL: Two. A boy and a girl.

MIRIAM: Oh, that's nice.

FRANCES: I'm sure they'll be fine.

HERB: Well, time to get on board.

> *(The others gather up their stuff. Phil doesn't move.)*

HERB: See you on board.

MIRIAM: Try not to take it so hard.

> *(The others get on. Phil doesn't move.)*

GATE AGENT: Sir, I'm afraid I'll have to ask you to board at this time. *(Pause.)* Sir, I'm afraid you have to —

PHIL: I've had a change of plans. I can't take this flight.

(He gathers up his things.)

GATE AGENT: I'm sorry sir, your ticket is only valid for this flight.

PHIL: That's all right. I'll make other arrangements. It happens. Can't be helped. Not your fault. I'll just call my —

GATE AGENT: This is the last flight out today.

PHIL: Well, I'm not getting on that plane and you can't make me!

GATE AGENT: Sir, if I have to, I will call Security.

PHIL: Go ahead.

GATE AGENT: I don't think you'd want me to do that, sir.

PHIL: Try me.

GATE AGENT: It could effect your ultimate destination.

PHIL: But it's not fair!

GATE AGENT: I understand.

PHIL: I'm too young. I've got so much to do.

GATE AGENT: I don't make the rules. I'm sorry. *(Pause.)* Now, if you'd please get on board.

(Phil concedes and goes to the door. He turns back.)

PHIL: Is there any kind of special last meal or anything?

GATE AGENT: There is beverage service and a snack on board.

PHIL: You mean, peanuts.

GATE AGENT: Yessir.

(Phil exits.)

GATE AGENT: This is your final boarding call.

(Lights fade to black.)

END OF PLAY

COPYRIGHT INFORMATION